LEAVING CUBA

FROM OPERATION PEDRO PAN TO ELIAN

KATHLYN GAY

TWENTY-FIRST CENTURY BOOKS
BROOKFIELD, CONNECTICUT

ACKNOWLEDGMENTS

A special thank-you is due Karen and Dean Hamilton and Arthur Gay for undertaking library research to find pertinent information on Cuban children of exile. I am also grateful to Karen Hamilton for her translations of Spanish documents. Pedro Pans who were especially generous with their time and information include Elly Chovel, Carlos Becerra, Mel Martinez, and Cesar Calvet. I appreciate also the help of foster parents Walter and Eileen Young of Sun City, Florida; social worker Tom Aglio of Orlando, Florida; Monsignor Bryan Walsh of Miami, Florida; Reverend Morton Park of Portland, Oregon; Sister Dorothy Jehle at Barry University in Miami Shores, Florida; and Esperanza B. de Varona at the Otto G. Richter Library of the University of Miami.

Gay, Kathlyn.
Leaving Cuba : from Operation Pedro Pan to Elian / Kathlyn Gay.
p. cm.
Includes bibliographical references and index.
Summary: Considers the various ways children have escaped from Communist Cuba and found refuge in the United States through different plans set up to help them, from the early 1960s to today.
ISBN 0-7613-1466-0 (lib. bdg.)
1. Refugee children—Cuba—Juvenile literature. 2. Refugee children—United States—Juvenile literature. 3. Refugee children—Services for—United States—Juvenile literature. [1. Cuban Americans. 2. Refugees.] I.Title.
HV640.5.C9 .G39   2000   362.87'083'0973—dc21   99-462149

Photographs courtesy of Kathlyn Gay: pp. 7, 27, 33; Archive Photos: p. 13; AP/Wide World Photos: pp. 18-19, 78-79, 92, 99, 107, 112, 117 (both); © *Miami Herald*: p. 38; UPI/Corbis-Bettmann: pp. 40-41, 65; Cesar Colvet: p. 55; Oregon Historical Society: p. 60; © Nik Wheeler/Corbis: p. 72; U.S. Coast Guard: p. 81. Map by Jeff Ward.

Published by Twenty-First Century Books
A Division of The Millbrook Press, Inc.
2 Old New Milford Road
Brookfield, Connecticut 06804
www.millbrookpress.com

CONTENTS

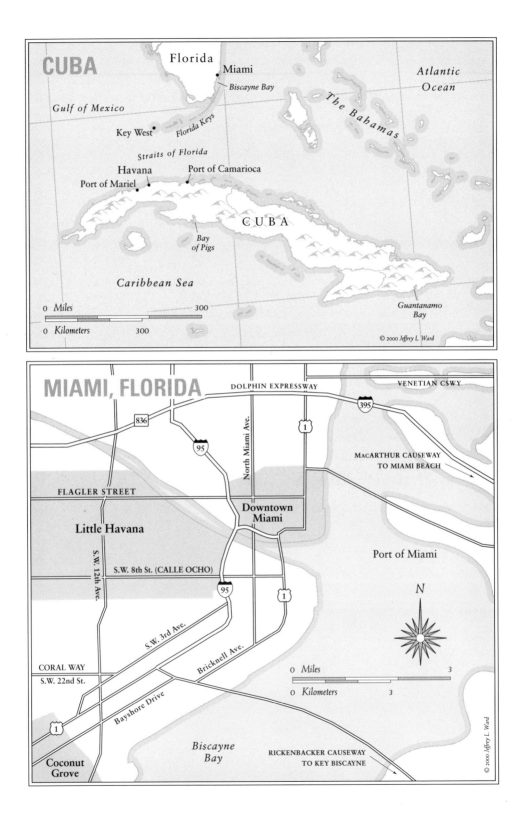

CUBA

Florida

Miami

Biscayne Bay

Atlantic
Ocean

Gulf of Mexico

The Bahamas

Key West

Florida Keys

Straits of Florida

Havana

Port of Camarioca

Port of Mariel

C U B A

Bay
of Pigs

Caribbean Sea

Guantanamo
Bay

0 Miles   300

0 Kilometers   300

© 2000 Jeffrey L. Ward

MIAMI, FLORIDA

DOLPHIN EXPRESSWAY

VENETIAN CSWY

836

395

95

North Miami Ave.

1

MacARTHUR CAUSEWAY
TO MIAMI BEACH

FLAGLER STREET

Downtown
Miami

Little Havana

Port of Miami

S.W. 12th Ave.

S.W. 8th St. (CALLE OCHO)

95

1

N

S.W. 3rd Ave.

CORAL WAY

Bricknell Ave.

0 Miles   3

S.W. 22nd St.

0 Kilometers   3

Bayshore Drive

1

Coconut
Grove

Biscayne
Bay

RICKENBACKER CAUSEWAY
TO KEY BISCAYNE

© 2000 Jeffrey L. Ward

INTRODUCTION

"I was terrified. Traveling alone to a strange place, without family or friends ... "

"I thank God every day that I was able to get to the United States safely. But I can't imagine sending my teenager let alone my seven-year-old to another country by herself where she couldn't speak the language and would be among strangers!"

"As teenage boys we thought it would be like a vacation or an adventure, flying from Havana, Cuba, to the United States. We expected to be back home within a few months."

These are typical of the kinds of comments that Cuban Americans, now in their forties or fifties, have made as they recall their exodus from Cuba, the island nation just ninety miles from Key West, Florida, the southernmost part of the United States. After Fidel Castro seized power in Cuba in 1959 and began to impose his Communist ideology on the Cuban population, more than 14,000 Cuban young people became part of what news reporters in the early 1960s eventually dubbed "Operation Pedro Pan." The name stems from the Sir James M. Barrie play *Peter Pan*, about the legendary boy who could fly and taught his friends to fly away with him to Never-Never Land.

At least once a year hundreds of Pedro Pan "alumni" in south Florida gather to recall the day they became children of exile, a day that some have described as the saddest in their lives. On occasion they try to express the overwhelming loneliness they felt leaving their families and homeland and discovering not long after they got to the United States that they could not return to Cuba within weeks or months. No one expected that years would go by before they would see their families again. Some never were reunited with their parents.

Over the centuries, since the time Christopher Columbus claimed the island of Cuba for Spain in 1492, the Cuban people have suffered under the harsh rule of dictators, and countless numbers have escaped to live in exile or have revolted and fought for Cuban democracy and freedom. In recent history, since 1959, well over one million people have legally left Cuba to live in exile, according to Professor Juan Clark of Miami Dade Community College. In his words: "It has been a very painful exodus, tragically dividing most Cuban families. Those who have sought to go into exile have first suffered discrimination and persecution at home. They have been sent to forced labor camps and [robbed] of all their property. Those who have remained behind are now encouraged to ask for dollars from their relatives abroad to buy in Cuba vital goods not available otherwise."[1]

The Pedro Pan flights of the early 1960s made up one of several mass migrations from Cuba that took place over four decades. People from all walks of life—

Operation Pedro Pan

Photos of some of the participants in Operation Pedro Pan are displayed at the annual alumni banquet in November 1998.

young and old—have fled Cuba, most seeking refuge in the United States. After the Pedro Pan airlifts, additional flights and then boat lifts from Cuba, particularly the 1980 Mariel boat lift that included many unaccompanied children (those without parents or guardians to live with) as the U.S. government labeled them, brought tens of thousands more refugees to south Florida. Since the 1960s, thousands of *balseros* (rafters)—some with children—have risked their lives in flimsy rafts to get to U.S. shores from Cuba.

In the summer of 1994 with Castro's tacit approval more than 35,000 Cubans left their homeland in crude rafts and homemade boats. The dictator hoped to rid the island of dissenters. According to the United Nations (UN), in 1994 about twenty-five people left Cuba each day, but at least six of that number died as they tried to escape across the dangerous Straits of Florida. Most rafters preferred to risk death rather than live under a repressive system that denied them their freedom and that made opposition seem futile.

Stories of Cuban exiles—children and adults—have filled the pages of numerous books, and have been the subject of hundreds of newspaper features over the years. TV documentaries and films have shown some of the desperate measures Cuban refugees have taken to find freedom. What is less publicized, however, is the continued imprisonment, torture, and assassination of those who dare to speak out against the Castro regime. The Cuban government does not allow such information to be released, but ex-prisoners and members of opposition groups who have formed a coalition called Concilio Cubano (Cuban Council) take great risks to get reports out to the world about the suffering of the Cuban people.

Hundreds of thousands of Castro's political opponents have been jailed or killed. Today Cuba has the highest number of political prisoners per capita of any country in the Western Hemisphere. Although the human rights organization Amnesty International (AI) reported in 1999 that the number of political prisoners in Cuba had decreased from the previous year, the organization expressed concern regarding

the number of critics of the Cuban Government who continue to be detained, harassed and threatened because of their peaceful attempts to exercise their rights to freedom of expression, association and assembly. Over the past year... dozens of members of unofficial groups, including human rights defenders and journalists, have been detained for short periods and threatened with being brought to trial if they do not give up their activities or go into exile. A handful have been convicted and some are still awaiting trial. Trials in political cases continue to fall short of international fair trial standards, particularly with regard to access to defence counsel. Defendants in cases heard by municipal courts, often only hours or days after arrest, sometimes have no legal representation whilst detainees held under investigation on state security charges often have only very limited access to lawyers while in pre-trial detention at police stations or at State Security headquarters. Detainees are sometimes subjected to psychological pressures, such as solitary confinement, long intense interrogations, threats and insults.[2]

Many Cuban exiles in the United States and else-where work with not only AI but also with other groups attempting to gain the release of political prisoners as well as prisoners of conscience (people jailed for their religious convictions). Cuban exiles also make tremendous efforts to stay in touch with and help support family members in their homeland, sending them American dollars and up to $800 million annually in food and medicine.

Thousands of Cuban exiles still want to go back home. If they could they "would go back yesterday," as is commonly expressed, because they had never planned to stay in the United States. In fact, some have lived for years with the belief that Castro would fall from power at any time and they could safely return home. Still other exiles say they are not sure they can ever go home again to live, primarily because they have become "Americanized" and now have children of their own; if those children were uprooted to move to Cuba, they (like their parents before them) would be strangers in a foreign land.

Only a few of the experiences of Cuban children of exile are included in this book, but they represent the tens of thousands involved in mass migrations for more than forty years. They also clearly show that countless exiled Cubans as well as Cubans in their homeland continue to hope and work for freedom.

CHAPTER 1

UPHEAVALS IN CUBA

Since the time of Spain's imperial domination of Cuba, which lasted from the 1500s to the late 1800s, Cuban rebels and freedom lovers have staged periodic insurrections and fought bloody battles to rid their country of colonial rulers and oppressors. After the Spanish-American War of 1898 brought freedom from Spanish rule, Cuba was still forced to accept conditions that made the nation dependent on the United States.

To achieve "independence," Cuba had to agree to the Platt Amendment, named for Senator Orville H. Platt of Connecticut, chairman of the Committee on Cuban Relations. The legislation authorized the president of the United States to withdraw troops from Cuba only if Cuba agreed to refrain from making any treaties that would impair its independence; not borrow any more money than it could repay; allow the United States to buy or lease land for naval bases; and permit the United States to intervene in Cuban affairs in order to maintain Cuban independence. Those stipulations, which were strongly opposed by Cubans, were attached to the nation's constitution.

Many members of the U.S. Congress questioned the legality of passing a bill to regulate a foreign country. Platt justified the amendment on the grounds that Congress had authorized intervention in Cuba with military action during the Spanish-American War, thus Congress, in Platt's view, had the right to determine when and how the troop occupation would end.

For decades the Platt Amendment was a source of contention between Cuba and the United States and helped lay the groundwork, many historians say, for turbulent times in Cuban politics. After a popular revolt in 1933, the Platt Amendment was revoked. However, political unrest continued and seven presidents ruled the country over the next few years. Behind the scenes, Fulgencio Batista amassed power and made himself a colonel and commander in chief of the army. By the 1950s, with the help of the Communist party, he was in control as dictator—terrorizing, jailing, killing, or deporting opponents.

During the 1950s, Fidel Castro and a band of other rebels formed a group to fight against Batista. The rebels attacked an army barracks on July 26, 1953, but their mission failed and Castro was imprisoned. Although he was sentenced to fifteen years, he was released two years later under a general amnesty, which Batista granted to many political prisoners in an effort to gain public favor.

Castro went to Mexico, where he trained a disciplined guerrilla force and helped form the *Movimiento 26 de Julio* (26th of July Movement), named for the barracks attack. The movement called for redistribution of land to peasants, mass education, nationalization of industries and public services, and the restoration of the 1940 constitution that embodied many political and social reforms, including democratic elections. Castro returned to Cuba in 1957 to work with various resistance groups opposing Batista, and by the following year the promise of a new democratic period seemed at hand.

Batista was forced to flee Cuba on January 1, 1959, and Fidel Castro and his guerrillas took over the government. They left the mountain encampment on the eastern end of the island, and wearing their rosaries, they paraded in their olive-green uniforms through the streets of Havana, the capital city. As syndicated columnist Roger Hernandez recalls, "That was January 8, 1959, one day before my fourth birthday, and sitting on my father's shoulders to welcome the 'saviors' along with tens of thousands other Cubans lining the parade route is one of my earliest memories."[1]

Fidel Castro and his troops were greeted as heroes as they paraded through Havana after taking over the government in January 1959.

To the vast majority of Cubans and many U.S. citizens, Castro was indeed a hero for a time. Catholic Church officials in Cuba had high hopes that a new "Christian spirit" would prevail.[2] Throughout most of 1959 the U.S. media and federal officials, including U.S. President Dwight Eisenhower, praised Castro, who made himself premier of Cuba and self-styled maximum leader of 6.5 million people. However, by the end of 1959, Cubans and Americans alike were becoming painfully aware that Castro had betrayed the revolution; the promised social justice and free elections in Cuba were not materializing. Indeed, revolutionary courts condemned hundreds of Batista followers to death and executed thousands who had supported Castro in the revolution but later questioned or defied his authority.

By early 1960, officials in Castro's totalitarian regime controlled most of the media—newspapers, radio, and television—and Communist propaganda was being circulated throughout the island. Academic freedom came to an end, and Castro forced the resignation of university professors who did not support his cause. He also banned independent student governments on campuses, and as a result a popular student, Pedro Luis Boitel, had to withdraw as a candidate for the national student council presidency, although students at five of the thirteen universities voted for Boitel anyway. A year later the Cuban government sentenced Boitel to a long prison term for "antirevolutionary" crimes. During the 1970s, Boitel went on a hunger strike in prison and died.

Private enterprise became a crime in Cuba, and Castro's government confiscated land and businesses. J. F. Everhart, a cattle rancher in Cuba who maintained his U.S. citizenship but had lived in his adopted homeland for twenty-five years, lost two ranches covering nearly 20,000 acres. The land was seized by Vidal Gil, a man who had once been Everhart's day laborer. Gil appeared with a revolutionary army captain and some soldiers and not only appropriated the land but also took all of the equipment, machinery, about three thousand head of cattle, and all the income from the ranches. According to Everhart's report at the time, his employees were told that the land

> would be turned into a "model co-operative" farm. Castro's National Institute of Agrarian Reform, or INRA ... has organized more than 600 "co-operatives" in Cuba so far. The peasants who belong to the "co-operatives" don't own any land of their own. The INRA holds the title. The peasants work the land at day wages, with the promise of a share in any future profits.[3]

Other Cuban landowners and businesspeople told similar stories that were published in the U.S. media. Articles also began to appear describing attacks on Protestant and Roman Catholic clerics and churchgoers in Cuba. Many were forced to leave the country. Some were sent to concentration camps, thrown in jail, or executed. Within a short time after Castro's takeover, U.S. government officials charged that Castro and his government were increasingly associating themselves with Communist countries, particularly the Soviet Union and China, and were launching a drive to spread communism throughout Latin America.[4]

CHILDREN IN DANGER

During 1960 and 1961, rumors throughout Cuba and news reports in the United States warned that Castro would make "every [Cuban] child a virtual ward of the state."[5] One article claimed that Castro required all public and private school students to "give written answers to questions about their family. Children must list the number and kind of books and newspapers their parents read, the kind of auto owned, and say whether the family has a radio, television, and refrigerator. Other questions deal with the beliefs and social life of parents."[6]

Rumors also circulated about Castro's plans for government nurseries—dormitories for children age three to ten—where children would be kept separated from their families. Stories told of one thousand Cuban youths sent to Russia to study collective farming methods and about "youth communes" set up in Cuba where young people from the age of ten would be housed, fed, and educated away from their parents and taught to be farmers.[7]

Most of the rumors proved to be based on fact. The Cuban government took over the educational system, which was and still is an effective way to indoctrinate students. Teachers are required to be watchdogs, government agents who keep a yearly Cumulative Academic Record documenting student grades and conduct and also "political integration"—loyalty to the regime as demonstrated through ideological and political activities.

> Any blot on the Cumulative Record means the student is guilty of political misconduct and could be refused access to higher education or the right to choose a career. The privileged careers, those with "social impact," are normally reserved for the "integrated." And finally, high school students are required to do "voluntary" farm work at the "schools in the countryside."[8]

Alfredo Lanier, who was a Cuban exile at the age of fourteen and in his adult years became a member of the Chicago Tribune editorial board, recalled a rumor that especially frightened Cuban parents: A statue in Russia honored a "young Communist child who had publicly denounced his counterrevolutionary parents." In later years Cuban exiles confirmed that as students in Cuba they were required to inform against their parents.

Lanier's parents were among those who lost their livelihoods. In June 1961 his father's printing shop and stationery store were confiscated by the government. As he explained further:

> My mother, a public school teacher, also was fired for not showing sufficient revolutionary zeal.
>
> In the modest middle-class neighborhood where we lived, our friends also were disappearing, as if stricken by a plague, selling off everything in their homes and furtively leaving town at night. As if to accelerate the exodus, a government vigilante group had set loudspeakers about a block away from our house, blaring a scratchy version of the Internationale [Communist anthem], over and over, 24 hours a day, for weeks on end.[9]

Another Cuban exile in Chicago, Hugo Chaviano, confirmed that parental concerns about forced indoctrination were very real. He wrote:

> I, for one, witnessed the nationalization of the Catholic school I attended through 3rd grade, Colegio de Belen, Fidel Castro's alma mater. I witnessed this school taken over by Army troops

and saw the Jesuit congregation, who owned and operated the school, kept under siege during the school's occupation. Ultimately, its priests, who served as teachers, coaches, and spiritual counselors, were expelled.

I attended Castro's public school system through the 7th grade and witnessed the communist indoctrination. I witnessed the peer pressure kids endured to become "Pioneros," or young pioneers, and later "Jovenes Comunistas," or young communists. I witnessed the requirement of having to "volunteer" to work on the countryside as part of your requirement to go on to the next grade. I also know children who were taught to view the revolution as their ultimate master and to tell on their parents if they thought they were engaged in "counter-revolutionary" activities.

Beginning in 1965 ... males between the ages of 15 and 27 years old were considered to be of military age and prohibited from leaving the country. This was the catalyst to my parents sending me out of the country.[10]

As it became clear that Castro would continue to ruthlessly impose his doctrines on the people, many wealthy and middle-class Cuban families left their country. *Time* magazine reported in August 1960:

Each weekday morning, when the doors of the U.S. consulate in Havana open, a long line of Cubans waits to enter. Their aim: to get out of Castro's Cuba. The consulate issues 200 visas a day, but the demand is so great that applicants now must wait [for months] even to get appointments for interviews. The drain on Cuba's supply of trained men—engineers, economists, doctors—persuaded Castro to cancel all existing exit permits. Henceforth, those who want to leave home must fill out an elaborately detailed questionnaire. Its aim was plain; to keep tabs on those who are getting out and to provide a handy list of their assets in case they do not come back.[11]

About 60,000 Cuban exiles fled to the United States during 1960, with a reported 30,000 to 40,000 finding refuge in Miami, Florida, by the end of the year. Among the first refugees were children whose parents were involved in counterrevolutionary underground efforts to depose Castro. Many of these parents feared that Castro's henchmen might take their children as hostages in order to force counterrevolutionaries to reveal themselves. Parents also worried that their teenage children might join anti-Castro youth organizations, putting their own and their families' safety and lives in jeopardy. Like Chaviano's parents, others were concerned that their sons would be drafted into the army. Thus, many parents believed the best way to protect their children was to send them to the United States through what was then the secret phase of Operation Pedro Pan. They trusted that their children would be cared for in the Cuban Children's Program initiated in Miami.

Background: By the fall of 1960, many Cubans had become disenchanted with Castro's rule. This photo taken at the U.S. Embassy shows a long line of Cubans seeking faster visas to flee the country.

CHAPTER 2

PEDRO, A PRIEST, AND A PLAN

Pedro Menendez had no knowledge about a whimsical flying character named Peter Pan when as a young teenager he became an exile in Miami, Florida. Instead his feet were flat on the ground, and he was suddenly thrust into what was for him the harsh reality of a new life. Because of concerns about Communist indoctrination, Pedro's parents in Cuba had sent their son to the United States to stay with relatives, also Cuban exiles, who lived in Miami. However, the relatives did not have the money to adequately feed, house, and clothe themselves let alone another family member, so Pedro was shifted from one relative's or friend's home to another, until he eventually found himself homeless, hungry, and very frightened. That's how he appeared in November 1960 when a benefactor took him to the Catholic Welfare Bureau (CWB) in Miami, hoping the agency could find a foster home for Pedro.

At the time, Father Bryan O. Walsh, a thirty-year-old Catholic priest born and reared in Ireland, headed the

CWB (later called Catholic Charities), a small child-care and adoption agency. Walsh, who eventually became a monsignor and is now retired, was able to find temporary care for Pedro. Yet Walsh was well aware that the boy's case was not an isolated one.

AN OVERWHELMING PROBLEM

Because Miami was the most accessible port of entry for refugees, social service agencies in the area, especially Centro Híspano Católico that served Spanish-speaking newcomers, had been experiencing a steady influx of Cuban exiles in need of help. "Community leaders quickly recognized that the problem was beyond their capacity to solve and appealed to the federal government [for help]," Walsh reported.[1]

In November 1960, before he left office, President Dwight D. Eisenhower sent Tracy Voorhees, who had overseen an earlier Hungarian refugee program, to assess the Miami situation. As a result, $1 million for emergency aid was provided, and a Cuban Refugee Emergency Center was set up in Miami. Voorhees recommended that some of the federal funds be used—if private resources were not available—to help "Cuban refugee children in extreme need," as his report put it.[2]

Although some of the earliest émigrés in late 1959 and early 1960 were wealthy or middle-class families able to bring funds and other resources to support themselves, by the mid-1960s Castro's government restricted the amount of money and personal belongings people could take out of the country. Many came with only a few dollars and a change of clothing.

DEVELOPING A PLAN

The plan to get endangered children out of Cuba actually began when two men agreed to work together—Reverend Walsh and James Baker, headmaster of Ruston Academy, a private American school in Havana. Although a U.S. citizen, Baker and his family considered Cuba home, and he became involved in efforts to protect children of underground activists. In December 1960 he went to Miami to meet with business leaders whose companies had been nationalized—taken over by Castro's government—hoping the businessmen would provide funds to set up a boarding school or other facility in the United States for refugee children. When Baker learned that the Catholic Welfare Bureau also had plans for child refugees, he went to see Walsh.

During that meeting, Walsh conveyed to Baker his conviction that "only licensed child-placing agencies should care for unaccompanied refugee children," and pointed out the importance of planning for the "total care of the child, including the legal questions of custody, which were bound to come up sooner or later." He also noted that "some children, especially the younger ones, belonged in foster families, not in institutions . . . [and] that the question of religious heritage would be very important in the minds of most Cuban parents, Jewish and Protestant, perhaps even more than Catholics, if the separation should prove to be lengthy."[3]

Baker had no argument with the priest's concerns. With the help of federal government officials, he and Walsh devised a basic plan to fly children out of Cuba. As Walsh explained:

The American embassy in Havana would be asked to grant a student visa. This would require proof that someone would be responsible for the child while in the United States and that the child was actually enrolled in a U.S. school. The Catholic Welfare Bureau attempted to meet these requirements by giving a letter to Mr. Baker for the U.S. Embassy accepting responsibility for any child designated by him and also by making arrangements to have [an immigration form] completed . . . for each child as proof of enrollment.[4]

Another part of the exit plan, soon to be labeled Operation Pedro Pan, was for Baker and Walsh to communicate through diplomatic sources. Secrecy was essential in order to protect Cuban families and to assure that Castro would not detain the children. Forms and letters plus funds provided by U.S. businessmen were sent through diplomatic channels to Baker in Cuba. Baker in turn sent a list of children ready to emigrate and to come under the care of the Cuban Children's Program, which was set up as a completely separate department of the Catholic Welfare Bureau in Miami. About two hundred children were expected; no one realized that the number would quickly grow and thousands would soon be Pedro Pan participants.

INITIATING OPERATION PEDRO PAN

After Baker returned to Cuba, Walsh and his staff could do little except wait to see how many children would come. They had few resources because federal funds would only be available after the children were under the agency's care. Housing was a major concern. There was a small group home operated by the CWB, and a group of vacant buildings once used by the County Welfare Department, which offered them to CWB in an emergency. Nevertheless, Walsh was confident he could count on Catholic Charities agencies throughout the United States to find homes for children, if that became necessary.

Then in early morning, December 24, 1960, Walsh received a call from a U.S. State Department official, telling him that a group of unaccompanied Cuban children would be able to leave their country and would arrive the next morning at the Miami airport. How many would arrive? No one knew. There could be two or twenty or the expected two hundred. So what was the priest to do? His staff was gone for the long holiday weekend. He had to have beds, food, and other basic necessities ready for the children. He quickly set out to make arrangements with a Catholic girls' boarding school, empty for the holiday break, to take in Cuban children at least until classes resumed in January. He also worked out overnight accommodations for about a dozen boys at St. Joseph's Villa, a Catholic institution for children. Finally on Christmas Day he was able to contact Louise Cooper, a social worker on his staff, to go with him to meet the young exiles at the airport. But after hours of waiting for flights, Walsh and Cooper faced disappointment. None of the expected Cuban young people arrived.

The next day, December 26, was a different story. Cooper went to the airport while Walsh continued making arrangements for housing. A late-night flight from Cuba brought two young exiles: Sixto and Vivian Aquino. When the brother and sister were taken under the care of Walsh's agency, the Cuban Children's

Program officially began and Operation Pedro Pan—the plan invented by Baker and Walsh—appeared to be working.

Over the next few days twenty more Cuban children flew to the United States and came under the care of Walsh's program. In addition, unaccompanied young people from Cuba, who had arrived in Miami earlier as tourists and had been staying with friends, also were taken in. But where were all the expected youths with student visas? Walsh soon found out. The U.S. Embassy in Cuba would not issue student visas unless "a recognized and established organization in the United States would . . . assume ultimate responsibility for the children." Since the CWB was a licensed child-care agency, it was acceptable to the Department of State, but, as Walsh reported, federal officials needed "an unconditional statement . . . accepting this responsibility."5

Walsh sent off the statement immediately. He was concerned that if he did not act at once, a new law would go into effect in Cuba on January 1, 1961. According to reports, the law would prevent the exodus of Cuban children. However, Castro had other ideas. He ordered the U.S. Embassy in Havana to cut its staff from 120 to 15 people. Within two days, the United States severed diplomatic relations with Cuba and closed the embassy in Havana. U.S. diplomats and many U.S. citizens, headmaster Baker and his family among them, returned to the United States.

Would Operation Pedro Pan be grounded? That seemed certain, but hopes soared once again when the British Embassy in Havana provided visas to send children to Kingston, the capital of Jamaica, at the time a British possession in the West Indies (Jamaica became independent in 1962). The young people, who were provided with transit visas, could then travel on to the United States. While all of these arrangements were being made, Walsh consulted with State Department officials and received assurances that Cuban children would be admitted to the United States by way of Kingston and also directly from Havana on special visa waivers. The waivers would be distributed in Cuba to children between the ages of six and sixteen. Sixteen to eighteen-year-olds could be admitted if they obtained security clearances from Washington, D.C.

The many meetings and telephone calls between government officials, airline managers, immigration authorities, and Walsh and his staff—and "countless prayers," as Monsignor Walsh would say—got Operation Pedro Pan moving again. The operation required the cooperation of U.S. voluntary organizations, the state of Florida, the federal government, and international operatives in a complex network that each week brought dozens and then hundreds of young Cubans to the United States for foster care. The U.S. government never before had funded foster care for refugee children. When news spread throughout Cuba that a U.S. government-funded program would save children from "Communist indoctrination," thousands of Cuban parents tried to get their children out.[6]

"It was something that my family never wanted to do," recalled Cesar Calvet, now a senior vice president at the SunTrust Bank in Orlando, Florida. But his parents felt they had little choice when Castro's regime began televising trials and executions. "I watched the firing squads on TV," Calvet said. "I was left with a very empty feeling" but a feeling that he could not adequately explain. "I guess at fifteen years of age I was too young to understand."

During the 1960s, newspapers carried numerous stories about Cuban children of exile.

Calvet pointed out that only after he became an adult could he really comprehend the great sacrifice his parents made. "I, at times, place myself in the shoes of my parents and do not know if I would be willing to send my children away. . . . I commend them for having the courage to do so . . . Pedro Pan saved a lot of us . . . from the possibility of being brainwashed and then supporters of the Communist regime."[7]

SEPARATION

When they talk about their experiences as Pedro Pans (which is how many adults still refer to themselves), they frequently describe a mixture of emotions that engulfed them as they were about to leave their country. "I was very afraid," Willy Chirino, now a renowned salsa musician, told a reporter during a Pedro Pan reunion in 1992. "It was the first time I was apart from my family. It was a shock for a schoolboy." Chirino wrote and recorded a song, "Nuestro Dia Ya Viene Llegando" (Our Day Is Coming), that tells the story about his departure from Cuba; the single was released in mid-1992 and soon became a hit in both Cuba and the United States.[8]

One of the most frightening procedures for young emigrants was going into the "fishbowl" or "fish tank," as it was called—a glass-enclosed room at the Havana airport. This was where airline passengers were herded; others were not allowed to enter.

"It was very scary," recalled Cesar Calvet. "We were subject to searches by the military." Cuban officials rummaged through duffel bags and suitcases, tried to take away youngsters' dolls, baseball gloves, and other treasured items, and in general played the bullies. In some cases, they told children they had to pay their telephone bills before they could leave, but of course they had no bills in their names. Relatives simply shoved money into children's hands and told them to pay whatever the guards demanded.

Some parents who were aware of the Cuban guards' extortion methods took precautions beforehand. One tactic was to hollow out the heel of a shoe and conceal money inside. Another was to sew coins or jewelry into clothing. As Elly Chovel, now a real estate agent in Coral Gables, Florida, recalled, "My mother sewed a little ring, which had been a birthday gift, inside a hem."

Chovel was sixteen years old when she and her twelve-year-old sister, Maria, boarded a plane for Miami. "I was scared, sad, and worried about what would happen to us when we arrived," she said. "I felt an awesome responsibility toward my younger sister. We were told when we got to Miami to say we were waiting for George—that was our code. George Guarch was indeed a real person, an employee of the Catholic Welfare Bureau who picked up the unaccompanied children daily at Miami's airport."9 Guarch then took his charges to foster-care centers.

Once on an airplane and flying toward the United States, anxiety sometimes was replaced by excitement. Jose Pimienta of Portland, Oregon, explained:

> I was 14 years old when I left [Cuba] in 1962. Initially I was very happy to be coming to the U.S. I was always very pro U.S.—music, clothes, food, etc. I guess I didn't realize what the consequences or possible future I was going to encounter. 10

Alfredo Lanier also flew out of Cuba in 1962. He recalled:

> When the pilot announced we were out of Cuban airspace, the kids cheered. A woman in her 50s sitting next to me, though, sobbed quietly. I looked at her nervously and she told me: "You kids don't realize that we'll never see our country again." She probably never did.11

ALONE

Within a short time after their arrival in the United States, some Pedro Pans *did* worry about the possibility of never seeing their homeland or relatives again, even though there was a widely held expectation that their parents would soon join them. Thirteen-year-old Magda Ojeda had planned to travel to the United States with her mother, but Cuban authorities barred her parent's exit, saying her papers were not in order. Ojeda went on alone, assured that her mother would be on the next flight. But that did not happen, and more than three years passed before her parents were able to come to the United States. "I had this overpowering feeling of loneliness," she told a Texas reporter twenty-five years after her arrival. Ojeda tried to erase that period from her memory. "It was not a rough time," she said, "but there was such a feeling of ambivalence, of terror, the hurt from the fear of never seeing your parents again."[12]

That same kind of feeling hit Jose Pimienta. Although he'd been excited about his trip to the United States, when he "realized there was no choice of going back, I cried myself to sleep a few nights," he said.[13]

Carlos Becerra was ten-and-a-half years old when he left Cuba alone and landed in Miami with two sets of clothes in a suitcase. His mother had told him to look for a man at the airport who would be holding a sign with Carlos's name on it. As promised, the man was there, but today Becerra has no recollection of the man's identity. "I was only ten," he said. "I just didn't think about such things." In short, he trusted the adult to care for him.[14]

At first Becerra, now a California resident, went to an emergency foster home where "only English was spoken; two other foster kids spoke Spanish," he wrote. "After a night goes by then it hits you. You are so sad and so homesick you go into a shell. It's so difficult to explain the feeling.... I was 5½ years without my parents. I can only imagine how bad it had to be for them ...I am crying as I am writing," he explained.[15]

After two weeks, Becerra was transferred to Florida City Center, about thirty-five miles south of Miami, where a group facility had been set up. Through the Cuban Children's Program, Walsh had leased a block of apartments and hired houseparents, teachers, cooks, medical personnel, and other staff to care for approximately four hundred youngsters. This "camp" as it was usually called, was one of several transit centers where they would be housed until they could be placed elsewhere. Spanish-speaking social workers greeted and interviewed arriving refugees, and medical staff conducted thorough physical examinations.

The first facility of this kind consisted of three buildings in Kendall, Florida, owned by Dade County, where Miami is located; the county loaned the buildings to the Children's Program. Camp Matecumbe, once a summer retreat set amidst a 150-acre pine grove in the southern part of the county, was a third transit center. In addition, other permanent-type facilities were established in the downtown area of Miami. But the need for more foster care facilities grew as more and more young refugees arrived.

Agencies such as the Jewish Family and Children's Service and the nondenominational Protestant Children's Service Bureau in the Miami area helped find foster care for some children. For example, a small Methodist group home was able to provide for about a dozen young people. National private organizations, including Church World Service, Catholic Relief Services, the United Hebrew Immigrant Aid Society, and the International Rescue Committee, helped relocate Cuban refugees outside the Miami area.

When President John F. Kennedy took office in 1961, he ordered the federal Department of Health,

Education, and Welfare (HEW), as it was known then, to take responsibility for all Cuban refugee programs. Under the leadership of Abraham Ribicoff, secretary of HEW, the department's Children's Bureau made arrangements with the Florida Department of Public Welfare to pay private agencies for the costs of each young refugee's food, clothing, transportation, education, and other necessities. According to the chief of the Children's Bureau at that time, "The rates of payment from federal funds were set at $5.50 per day for foster-family care and $6.50 per day for institutional care."[16]

To find suitable foster homes, ads were placed in regional and national magazines. "The Need Is Desperate" one ad in the Toledo, Ohio, *Catholic Chronicle* stated, pointing out that none of the Cuban children could be adopted (custody remained with their parents in Cuba), and that

> Foster Parents will be given ample financial compensation.
> It is NOT necessary that applicants be a Spanish speaking family.
> Placement is for an indefinite period of time, i.e., until their parents can come to the U.S. and are gainfully employed.
> Children are 6 to 16 years of age.[17]

Articles in a variety of religious magazines called for help. *The Christian Century* put it this way:

> Many U.S. citizens traveling through Latin America have received the gracious Spanish welcome "Está usted en su casa." Now several hundred American families can return the hospitality

Monsignor Bryan Walsh (right) met with Abraham Ribicoff, secretary of the U.S. Department of Health, Education, and Welfare in the 1960s, to discuss the U.S. government's role in reimbursing private agencies for the costs of providing for young Cuban refugees.

each month, saying to Cuban children bereft of parents, "Make yourself at home!". . . . We can think of few better ways to "fight communism" than to care for the children who flee from it.[18]

By fall 1962, Pedro Pan refugees were "in foster care in 35 states under the auspices of 95 different child welfare agencies," Walsh reported.[19] Out of the 14,048 young people who had come to the United States through Operation Pedro Pan, more than 50 percent were helped through the Cuban Children's Program and its staff, which grew to more than 400 and included social workers, registered nurses, teachers, office personnel, houseparents, and domestic workers. Some of the staff were nuns and priests who were forced to leave Cuba after Castro nationalized Catholic schools and closed churches. About 1,300 young people were placed under other private and public care, while the remaining exiled Pedro Pans found shelter with relatives and family friends. Yet there were 50,000 young Cubans with visas still waiting to get out of their country. [20]

CHAPTER 3

CRISES AND RESENTMENTS

During the time that Operation Pedro Pan was under-way, a political war between the United States and Cuba was heating up. After Kennedy became president in 1961, he continued and enhanced the Eisenhower poli-cies aimed at aiding Cuban refugees. His administration tried to weaken Fidel Castro's regime with a "brain drain"—encouraging some of the brightest people in Cuba to leave. By establishing an open-door policy and funds for Cuban refugees, the U.S. government helped to bring about a mass exodus of physicians, lawyers, teachers, engineers, and other professionals from Cuba. "The exodus became so large, and its effects so damag-ing, that the Cuban government tried to stop the fleeing professionals by depriving them of their citizenship and prohibiting their return to their families in Cuba. When these measures failed to turn the tide, however, Castro tried to downplay the exodus, dismissing it as a mis-guided and mistaken decision that the exiles would some day regret."[1]

Kennedy also supported the previous administra-tion's plan to overthrow Castro by force. At a camp in Guatemala, the U.S. Central Intelligence Agency (CIA) began training 1,500 Cuban exiles for a military invasion of their homeland, expecting that Cubans on the island would rise up and join the troops. In April 1961 the U.S.-trained soldiers landed at Bahía de Cochinos (Bay of Pigs) on the south coast of Cuba. In three days Castro's soldiers defeated the invading force, capturing and imprisoning about 1,200 men.

The Bay of Pigs fiasco humiliated the United States, and not long after the failed mission, the CIA inspector general began an internal investigation, subsequently issuing a report that was highly critical of the operation. Stamped "top secret" for thirty-six years, the report was finally declassified in 1998 and posted on the Internet by the National Security Archive of George Washington University. Included in its 150 pages are stinging critiques, among them that the CIA did not have adequate information on the strength of the Castro regime. CIA operatives "failed to appraise the chances of success realistically...[and] to keep the national policy-makers adequately and realistically informed." The report also criticizes the operation as being "badly organized and without adequate assets in the way of boats, bases, training facilities," and other necessary items, and concluded that the CIA conducted an operation beyond its capability.[2]

CUBAN OPERATIVES

In spite of the bungled invasion, Castro did not stop flights between Havana and Miami, and young people continued to leave Cuba aided by a network of adults working in secret. One of the adults was Penny Powers, a British nurse. Powers had been instrumental during the late 1930s—just before World War II broke out—

helping Jewish children escape Nazi persecution through a British program called kindertransport. The British allowed only children under the age of sixteen to immigrate, and Jewish parents in Germany and Austria sent their children into exile before Nazis could herd them into concentration camps.

In Cuba, Powers worked with the nephew and niece of former Cuban president Ramón Grau San Martín—Ramón Grau Alsina and his sister Leopoldina Grau Aguero. Known by their nicknames Mongo and Polita, they secretly distributed waiver visas to help children get to the United States. To this day, many Pedro Pans speak of these two underground operatives in reverent tones, awed and thankful for their heroism.

Both Mongo and Polita were sentenced to prison in 1965 for counterrevolutionary activities; Polita was released after fourteen years and emigrated to Miami. Her brother spent more than twenty years in prison and for three months suffered torture in a tomblike cell twelve feet underground. Guards wanted Grau to give them names of people involved in the Pedro Pan exodus so the operatives could be sent to the firing squad. In 1997 in a story for the *Miami Herald*, he described his cell, which had

> a concrete beam running across the ceiling that housed an air-conditioning duct. The height of the beam prevented me from walking erect or stretching. . . . The walls and the ceiling were painted in black with spots of hallucinating color. The concrete walls had a rough finish which tore the skin on contact and prevented rest. There were many microphones and speakers and a single light bulb behind a metal grid.

Ramón Grau Alsina (right) and his sister, Leopoldina Grau
Aguero, risked their lives to help Cuban children of
Operation Pedro Pan to get to the United States. After being
imprisoned by Castro for many years, they were released
and came to Miami. Ramón Grau died there in 1998,
Leopoldina Grau Aguero died in 2000.

When he was thrown into the cell, Grau had only a small metal cup and a handkerchief with him. He wore only his underwear, which he had had on for three months. In the cell he was subjected to the light and the air-conditioning being turned on and off at random intervals, causing

shocks of painful cold or heat, total darkness or unbearable brightness. Moaning sounds occasionally came through the speakers, but there were long periods of terrifying silence [that] magnified the feeling of being alive in a grave. Roaches and fleas used my body for exercise and food. A big rat ate part of my handkerchief. From time to time the lock and lever would screech, and a metal plate with corn meal would be tossed in from the dark and water would be poured into my cup.

One day a piece of bread with mayonnaise came flying in. The mayonnaise caused me to hallucinate....I began to sing opera ... the guards rushed in ...[and] took me to the lieutenant ... worried that I had become insane. The lieutenant demanded my confession. I asked him to return me to the hole, a request that he quickly granted.

I lost track of time before guards again opened that iron door and took me to the shower, where I found a thin film of soap. On a mirror nailed to the wall I also saw the reflection of what looked to be an 80-year-old man with a beard down to the waist. I was not even 40.[3]

The guards finally gave up on Grau. He was tried and received a death sentence that was commuted to twenty-three years in prison. In 1986 he was released and along with dozens of other political prisoners flew to Miami, where he became the elder statesman of the Cuban exile community. When he died in November 1998, just a few days before his seventy-sixth birthday, he was eulogized as a fighter for Cuba and democracy. His family cremated his body, hoping someday to take his ashes to a free Cuba.

A NUCLEAR THREAT

Young exiles in the United States knew nothing about Grau's story until much later in their lives. During the early 1960s, they believed that they would soon be going home. However, the Kennedy administration became increasingly concerned about Castro's ties with Nikita Khrushchev, Communist leader of the Soviet Union. Russian-made tanks, antiaircraft guns, and other military equipment were on display in Cuba. When Castro announced in September 1962 that Havana Harbor would become a major port for a Soviet fishing fleet, U.S. military officials declared the harbor would actually become a Russian naval base.[4] Then in mid-October, U.S. spy planes flew high over the island and took photographs that clearly showed Soviets constructing missile sites. Missiles with nuclear warheads were aimed at the United States.

Kennedy's military advisers recommended an invasion or air strikes on the missile sites and other targets across Cuba, but the president wanted to find other means to resolve this threat. On October 22 he ordered a navy "quarantine" (blockade) of Soviet shipments of military equipment to Cuba. The president deliberately substituted the term "quarantine" for "blockade," since the latter could be interpreted as an act of war.

Over the next six days, tensions mounted as Khrushchev accused Kennedy of pushing the world toward nuclear destruction and challenged the United States by declaring that Russia would ignore the quarantine. At sea Russian ships thought to be carrying missiles for Cuba came close to the quarantine line, but they did not cross it. The showdown came on October 28, when Khrushchev agreed to withdraw the missiles if

Kennedy promised not to invade Cuba and to remove U.S. missiles based in Turkey.

Because of the Cuban Missile Crisis, as it became known, all flights from Havana to the United States were terminated, ending Operation Pedro Pan, which had lasted for twenty-two months. Nevertheless, Castro could not totally block Cubans seeking refuge. Over the next two to three years, thousands of refugees made the trip across the treacherous Straits of Florida, primarily by small boats, or traveled to other countries—Spain and Mexico, for example—to get visas for travel to the United States. Most parents of Pedro Pans were unable to leave Cuba, however. The young people in exile had to go on with their lives in foster care, which for some was highly traumatic while for others was emotionally rewarding and a growing experience.

IN TRANSITION

On arrival in Miami, hundreds of Pedro Pans under the care of the Cuban Children's Program went to transit centers—group facilities and camps—set up by the Catholic Welfare Bureau. The young refugees were plunged into an environment that was quite different from their home atmosphere. Guillermo Cespedes, who eventually went to live in the San Francisco Bay area, came with a younger sister, and the two Pedro Pans found themselves somewhat conspicuous as dark-skinned Afro-Cubans. In Cespedes's view, "There was a lot of physical abuse and racism in the camp, which was new to me because I had been the pampered son and never experienced such treatment. In reaction and for self-protection, I became an angry young man." His three months in the transit center "seemed like an eter-

Background: The Cuban Missile Crisis, October 1962, was resolved when the Soviet Union agreed to withdraw its missiles from Cuba. This aerial photo of a departing Russian ship shows eight missile transporters with canvas-covered missiles.

nity." He ended up in Roxbury, Massachusetts, "close to being a juvenile delinquent," he told a news reporter. Yet he turned his life around and became the founder of Conjunto Cespedes, "the best known Afro-Cuban band outside of Cuba."[5]

Whether or not Cuban children felt the sting of racism, most who came through Pedro Pan had been pampered by their parents, who made their children the center of attention within their families. Some children had always been waited on by servants and were never expected to do chores such as making a bed or picking up clothes. Although most had been taught to obey their parents and other authority figures, the young people were not necessarily accustomed to the rules and regulations of camp or group facilities.

At Camp Matecumbe for adolescent boys, for example, a list of *Reglamentos* began with a "cordial welcome" and a wish that the camp would be a *segundo hogar* (second home) for the teenagers housed there. But it also pointed out that the camp was *tránsito* and that at any moment a boy or group of boys could be placed elsewhere. The rules of the camp and disciplinary measures applied to all, the *Reglamentos* stated. One rule required a daily shower at a scheduled time in the shower room, but to prevent accidents no one was allowed to use the shower at the Olympic-size swimming pool unless an instructor was present. Another regulation prohibited placing calls to Cuba from any telephone in the camp.

Everyone was restricted to the camp during weekdays, but a teenager could leave on weekends if an adult friend or relative personally came to the camp and assumed responsibility for him. As would be expected, it was "ABSOLUTAMENTE OBLIGATORIA" for boys to attend school classes. Finally, the list of instructions reminded them that they were in a Catholic camp and that their manner of talking and their behavior should reflect their religious teaching.[6]

When he was fifteen years old, Melquiades "Mel" Martinez spent forty-five days at Camp Matecumbe. Now a successful Orlando, Florida, attorney and elected Orange County chairman, Martinez says he is extremely grateful for having a "a good and fulfilled life" that includes a "wonderful wife and three children." His first year in the United States, however, "was very hard and it's difficult to talk about because you'd rather not remember."

Martinez was part of Operation Pedro Pan in 1962 when every week several hundred young Cubans flew to Miami. Boys between the ages of six and eighteen outnumbered girls by almost two to one in this exodus. Even though Martinez was surrounded by other teenagers like himself, he was still among "total strangers" and said he felt

> incredibly alone, like an orphan—quite a contrast to having lived in a nurturing kind of home in a small town in Cuba where everybody knew my family—my grandfather, my grandmother, my mother, and my dad. I had gone to one school all my life, the same school my dad had gone to. Then to land in Miami in a camp that had been built for about 120 but was crowded with about 450 kids in barrack type dorms ... They were so crowded that bunk beds were three layers high ... the guy on the top would kind of burn because the heat [vent] was at his level and the guy on the bottom would freeze. I remember

once a guy next to me coughing all night and we were so close together that I could feel his cough.7

For Martinez and other Pedro Pan boys arriving in 1962, the crowding and lack of privacy were often difficult to handle. Using communal showers and bathrooms was especially embarrassing for many. "You could sit on the toilet and people were always walking around."

As he tried to adjust to the camp situation, Martinez found a "saving grace"—organized baseball teams. "I went out for sports and I played baseball, which made me feel a little bit better." Still, the loneliness and homesickness did not subside completely. Then, after about a week or ten days at the camp, "one of the most wonderful things happened . . . . I ran into a man who was picking up trash—working around the place—and got to talking to him and he was nice enough to chat with me and somehow it turned out that he knew my dad—knew about my family some way. After that I just sort of clung to him, sought him out to talk to him."8

Of course not all Pedro Pans had the same experiences at transit facilities, and their reactions often depended on their age and length of stay. Hundreds were reunited with their parents or other family members within a few weeks or months. Among those who waited years for reunions, some had to be transferred from one facility to another. For example, when the borrowed Kendall facility had to be vacated in 1962 because of the county's need for the camp, young boys were moved to large empty barracks on a U.S. Marine base at Opa-Locka, Florida, northwest of Miami. When Matecumbe was closed in 1964, teenage boys were also moved to Opa-Locka.

Among the thousands of young exiles in group facilities were a small number who rebelled and tried to run away, or refused to learn or speak English because they insisted they would be going home soon. Others found their life at transit centers an adventure, "like going to summer camp." Nevertheless, the camps were "no way to live," as one Pedro Pan noted. Another, Maria Masud, who became a Spanish professor at DePaul University in Chicago, remembers that at the camp where she and her brother stayed "a lot of children had emotional difficulties."[9]

Caregivers were well aware that the children were homesick and lonely, but social workers and medical personnel maintained that for the most part children did not have severe psychological problems and adjusted quite well. Some teenage exiles, especially those from affluent families, had long expected to go to school in the United States, so they were somewhat prepared for the idea of being separated from their parents. Still, in later years dozens of Pedro Pans have reported psychological problems, such as fear of being alone, that they trace to their childhood experiences. Others have repressed their feelings for so long that they cannot talk about their early exile without dissolving into tears. Some had never discussed their childhood experiences until recent years. As Californian Carlos Becerra noted in mid-1998: "I just told my grown daughter for the first time about Pedro Pan."[10]

IMPACTS ON SOUTH FLORIDA

Even though Catholic and other religious groups in south Florida provided hundreds of thousands of dollars in aid for many Cuban refugees, the private sector alone was overwhelmed by the 200,000 newcomers in the Miami area during the three years between early 1960 and the end of 1962. Schools were especially hard hit. Children under the care of the Catholic Welfare Bureau attended school classes in camps or at Catholic schools nearby. Others attended public schools in the Miami-Dade County area, which operates under a combined metropolitan form of government. The Dade County school system was suddenly faced with enrolling thousands of young refugee students.

Joe Hall, then the Dade County superintendent of schools, noted in a 1962 report that Miami had long been a cultural and educational center for Spanish-speaking families, but the sudden influx of Cuban refugees from 1960 through 1962 created unexpected financial burdens, overcrowded conditions, and a great need for additional teachers in some schools. Yet the educational system met the challenges quite well, especially after the federal government provided financial aid. As Superintendent Hall reported, "It was apparent from the beginning of the influx of Cuban refugees into the Dade County area that this was a national problem and that financial support of the education of thousands of refugee children should not and could not be borne by the citizens of Dade County and of the State of Florida."[11]

Federal funds helped pay for special textbooks to teach English and the services of bilingual teacher aides, usually former teachers in Cuba, and also adult education programs for Cuban refugees. When the 1962–1963 school year began, more than 18,000 Cuban refugee children were in grades one through twelve, and more than 10,000 adult refugees were enrolled in adult education programs. Because of the Cuban Missile Crisis near the end of 1962, student enrollment dropped from around two hundred per week during October 1962 to just over fifty the last week of January 1963.[12]

The labor market in Miami-Dade County was also greatly affected by thousands of Cuban exiles. Some south Floridians claimed that refugees took jobs away from native-born workers. Yet studies conducted in the 1960s showed that at least during the decade that was not the case. Instead, because of federal subsidies, Cubans were able to contribute to Dade county's economy. Many established businesses—a *carniceria* (meat market), upholstery shop, pharmacy, used car lot, café, cigar shop, or just about any other kind of commercial operation imaginable. In fact, one commercial strip on Calle Ocho (Eighth Street) became the heart of what is known as Little Havana, a popular tourist attraction today.

Nevertheless, non-Cubans in Miami-Dade County began to express resentment during the early 1960s as federal funds for Cuban refugees provided ever-increasing benefits, from grants to resettle in areas where jobs were available to welfare relief, which was higher than the average American citizen received. Federal aid was not the only thing that created resentment. As history professor María Cristina García explained: "Miamians complained that their Spanish-speaking neighbors were boisterous, rude, and disrespectful of American laws, especially traffic regulations." Native Miamians disliked the Cuban driving habit of speeding through traffic blasting a horn rather than applying the brakes when needed. Other complaints included crowded housing.

Because of the housing shortage, many Cuban families temporarily moved in together, causing many Miamians to fear that property values would drop and slum districts similar to Spanish Harlem in New York City would be created. Signs reading "No Cubans allowed" became a common sight in apartment buildings throughout the city; others barred families with children from renting . . . . Blacks watched in disbelief as Cuban black and mulatto children attended "white schools," prompting one local minister to write that "the American Negro could solve the school integration problem by teaching his children to speak only Spanish."[13]

Local residents also expressed concern that Cuban exiles would use south Florida as a "base from which to launch their war against Castro. Several [Cuban] political organizations carried out paramilitary maneuvers against the island . . . and local authorities frequently confiscated large caches of munitions. Miamians feared for their security and resented being caught in the middle of someone else's war."[14]

Some of the negative stereotypes of Cubans followed young refugees who were relocated to other parts of the United States, particularly in areas where few Spanish-speaking people lived, such as the Midwest and Northwest. Because of prejudicial attitudes among Anglo Americans, one reporter from Madison, Wisconsin, was prompted to write an article describing the many attributes of Cuban young people. "Cuban girls," Lillian Nitcher wrote for the *Wisconsin State Journal*, "are quiet, well-mannered ladies whether they are 3 or 17." She pointed out that boys would be boys no matter where they went, "But a friend of mine in California tells me there are 30 Cuban kids in her school and they are 'wonderful.' "15

Cuban kids tried their best to be "wonderful" whether they went to Washington, Oregon, Wyoming, Indiana, Ohio, Michigan, or some other state. One young man wrote from his foster home in Indianapolis, Indiana, that he was among only a few Cuban refugees in the area, and "for sure we have produced a good impression here. [We] have made use of our good manners," which he explained had "perhaps been forgotten" when they were in the transit camp at Matecumbe.16

CHAPTER 4

MORE UPHEAVALS

When young Cuban exiles were sent to foster-care facilities outside Miami-Dade County, they had to face still another kind of adjustment—getting accustomed not only to cultural differences but also to geography and surroundings unlike any they had known before. Sixty Cuban refugee children were sent to the Sacred Heart Home in Pueblo, Colorado, for example. As adults they often recall the difficulty of not being allowed to speak Spanish and rejection by American children living there. Yet most also remember positive experiences and went on to the "good life" in later years.

Others, like Teresita Rodriguez, were assigned to a Catholic girls school in San Antonio, Texas. Teresita hated the idea of having to adjust to another new and strange environment, and her years at the school were very difficult, she told a reporter. The nuns in charge "got the idea that we were orphans. We were refugees. Our parents were in another country." According to a *Houston Post* story:

> As the months passed, Rodriguez began to think it was unlikely she would ever be reunited with

her parents . . . . Her father was a pediatrician, and she knew that for Communist Cuba, doctors were a valuable commodity.

Her parents, too, were having similar thoughts. A year and a half after her arrival, Rodriguez's parents appealed to the U.S. government to send their daughter back to Cuba. The request was denied.

Her parents never told Rodriguez about their request and the U.S. government's answer until they were reunited in Miami in April 1966. They wanted to spare her any additional pain.

If she could have done things differently . . . [she] "would have stayed in Cuba." Her thinking is based on personal and deep familial considerations—not politics. "My parents and I went through a lot."[1]

Elly Vilano Chovel had quite a different reaction to her move from south Florida. After three months in the Florida City transit camp, she and her younger sister went to a foster home in Williamsville, New York, near Buffalo. "The American family who welcomed us were kind and wonderful. I will always be grateful," she wrote. Still it is never easy to settle into a new environment. "We had to grow up in a hurry, be responsible. . . . The things you take for granted while living with your own family were instantly gone," she noted.

When she left Cuba, Elly was in her first year in high school, and she enrolled for her sophomore year in a Catholic high school in Williamsville. "Although it was difficult to learn quickly a new language, we were used to many hours of study with intense subjects European style. So the American school system was easier for us," she explained, adding that her education also included learning "about the customs and culture of other nationalities in the area—Polish, Irish, German, and Italian."

Elly and her sister stayed with their foster family for three-and-a-half years—until their mother and father, Carlos and Caridad Vilano, emigrated. "My parents were able to leave Cuba by going to Spain. My great-aunt got them a Spanish visa and after six months in Spain they got permits to join us in New York," she wrote.[2] The Vilanos and their two girls then moved to the Miami area where Chovel still lives and is a successful real estate broker. As president of the Operation Pedro Pan Group, Chovel spends much of her free time helping to organize events and responding to inquiries about Pedro Pan alumni.

FROM FLORIDA TO OREGON

After living in three different facilities in Florida—Florida City, Kendall, and Opa-Locka—between 1962 and 1965, Carlos Becerra was assigned to a foster-care program under the guidance of Reverend Morton Park in Portland, Oregon, as far removed from Miami by miles, climate, and culture as almost any U.S. location could be. For a time, Becerra lived in a two-story home called St. John's House that was supported by Catholic Charities (now Catholic Social Services). Foster parents were in charge of the household that included eight other foster teenagers. Becerra was by then (1965) in his first year in high school.

"I was the only Cuban [in the school] so some students had a hard time with that," he wrote. "I just had to kick some butt to make sure they knew I was no one that they could fool with. I've always been a fighter," said Becerra, who as an adult is trim, athletic, and full of energy. He also coaches a senior's softball team that plays in competition across the United States.

Becerra's love for sports prompted him to try out for his high school baseball team, but the coach let him know in no uncertain terms that

> no spic would ever play for him. What an idiot! This one guy gave me more motivation to become someone than any single person while I was growing up. I sent this guy my W-2 [tax form] for years afterward, letting him know how his "little spic" was making "strikes"—a better living than he as a teacher.[3]

In spite of such prejudices, Becerra has fond memories of other educators who inspired and helped him. He moved to another Portland home, where the man in charge happened to have been his physical education teacher in Cuba and knew him very well—"a happy coincidence," Becerra said. Attending another high school, Becerra met "a beautiful lady, Dorothy Morris, who taught non-English-speaking students—at one time we had 20 kids with 20 different languages. She taught them all. Within one year I could speak English very well."

In 1967 his parents were able to leave Cuba, and their arrival in Portland "was one incredible day in my life!" he said. His parents opened a grocery store in Portland but sold it in 1975 when they moved to California. Becerra also made California his home and after a brief time in the Marine Corps began a business career in a Ford dealership. "I'm now one of the most respected service directors in the business," he noted with obvious pride, adding that he credits his early childhood hardships with his tremendous desire to succeed. Getting through those years after coming to the United States without his parents were "rough times" but, he said, "Even today I could never be able to explain to my parents how much I love them for their incredible sacrifices and not being selfish and trusting God to guide us" through such an ordeal.[4]

A FOSTER-FAMILY STORY

Mel Martinez never left Florida, but he was assigned to a shelter far from Miami in the northern part of the state: Camp St. John's near Jacksonville. When he learned about his new placement, Martinez was elated—he knew he would be with friends from Cuba, one of whom was Cesar Calvet. The camp with ninety boys in residence was not paradise, however. In fact, it had been in a state of near chaos because of management problems until a young social worker, Tom Aglio from Massachusetts, came to oversee the camp.

Aglio, who later became director of Catholic Social Services of Orlando, readily admits that when he first arrived at St. John's, he was intimidated by the rebellious boys and was not sure whether he could handle the tremendous responsibility. He also had only a little understanding of the Spanish language, although some of his staff were Cuban Americans and helped with communication. Still, Aglio knew the boys needed to learn English in order to function outside the camp. Aglio decided early on to require that "whenever the boys spoke they had to use English or I wouldn't acknowledge them, I just wouldn't respond," he said.[5]

A group of Cuban refugee boys at Camp St. John's near Jacksonville, Florida

Yet this was part of a bluff, because he gave the impression that he could understand anything his charges said in Spanish. Only when he delivered a farewell speech in faltering Spanish did the boys discover the ruse; they rose to their feet, applauding and cheering.

Most boys in the camp came to love Aglio as a *padre segundo* (second father) and today remember that he made the camp feel like home. Nevertheless, the diocese decided to close camp St. John's and place the boys with foster families, certainly more suitable for growing teenagers but one more upheaval for them to face. It was Aglio's job to find suitable homes for everyone. Through articles in Catholic and other religious publications and calls from pulpits, families learned about the need for homes.

Among those who responded to the appeal were the Youngs—Walter, Eileen, and their two sons, Jim and Dennis—who lived near Orlando. They did not make this decision easily, however. At first her sons, ages fifteen and thirteen, were against the idea of sharing their home, bedroom, parents, friends, and other aspects of their lives with another teenager, a stranger at that. Eileen Young understood and was about to let Tom Aglio know that her family could not offer foster care. Before she could make a call to the social worker, however, her eldest son, Jim, speaking for himself and Dennis, said, "No, Mom, we've talked this over and we've decided there's no reason why we shouldn't have someone come." Their decision and the personality of the young man, Mel Martinez, who came to live with them made the situation work, Eileen Young said, because "it could have been a very big problem with two fifteen-year-olds in the house—jealousy, rivalry, all that—it could have been very competitive," she explained, "but it wasn't."

The Young family met Mel at the bus station in Orlando. "Sixty boys got off that bus with name tags on them," Eileen said, and families were there to pick up their charges. "Mel got in our car and the first thing we did was ask him how to pronounce his name: Melquiades Martinez—I kept saying MAR-tin-ez. I asked if we could call him Mel—which was fine—but he insisted on the correct pronunciation for his family name."

In the Young home, getting acquainted and learning about each other were the first important tasks. Jim and Dennis showed Mel around and got him settled in their bedroom. "Mel took one of the bunk beds with Dennis, and Jimmy took the studio couch in the Florida room [enclosed back porch]," Eileen explained. As Mel hung up his clothes in the closet, "all he kept saying was thank you, thank you, thank you, thank you. I finally told him no more 'thank you'—once is enough!" Eileen said. Then they went out to the kitchen where Eileen fixed Mel a peanut butter sandwich, thinking that was one way to make him feel at home. But Mel had never eaten such a sandwich before—it was not part of the Cuban cuisine.

Then there was the matter of how Mel should address Walter and Eileen Young. With the help of their son Jim, who knew some Spanish, Eileen asked Mel what he wanted to call her.

> He suggested "Mommy" and "Poppy" and I had to say oh, no, no, no you only have one Mommy and nobody will ever take the place of that one Mommy and I'm just a lady who is going to help your mother help you like I'd want someone to help my boy. So I asked Jimmy how to say 'aunt' in Spanish. 'Tia' Jim said. I became Tia and Walter became Tio—even our own children and nieces and nephews began calling us Tia and Tio and still do.

As the days and months passed, only a few adjustments had to be made in the household, both Eileen and Walter Young recalled. Food was probably one of the major concerns since the Youngs were used to a meat and potatoes diet. Potatoes, however, were no more popular than peanut butter. Eileen tried to cook rice and black beans the Cuban way, but the dish never turned out quite right.

She also had to explain to Mel that he was expected to help out with household chores. "One day Mel was drying dishes and he said 'if my Poppy saw me doing dishes, he would be mad.' I said, 'Oh, really? Let me tell you, you are here, you see my boys do dishes, you do dishes too. You're in Cuba you don't do dishes, but here you do. Your Poppy would tell you to do what has to be done to make it [life here] work.'"6

Eileen eventually became involved through Catholic Charities with many other young Cuban refugees, helping them find medical care, clothing, and other needed items. The Youngs also opened their home to Mel's brother, Rafael, when he arrived from Cuba, sent by his parents to stay with relatives in Miami. Rafael, who later became an attorney, went to Orlando for visits and summed up those experiences in a letter he addressed to "Dear Tia and Tio" on their fiftieth wedding anniversary in 1995:

> I recall those summers when you invited me to Orlando to spend weeks with you. Aside from your great generosity to Mel, you were very generous to me. I look back to how important those years were for my formation as a young adult in America. I recall how I admired both of you and looked up to you . . . .
>
> I remember Tia's kindness towards me at a . . . time in my life without my parents. You filled a great vacuum for me, Tia . . . . Having come from Cuba at the age of twelve without my par-

ents, I had to grow up very fast. It was fun coming to Orlando and being the youngest in the group and having you pamper me like I was a little one. I'll never forget, Tia, how perceptive you were when it came time for me to leave. You knew that my suitcase was pretty empty and knowing that we didn't have the money to buy clothes, you would always stuff a couple of T-shirts or shorts in from your kids . . .

Both of you have continued to be great role models and loving friends through the years . . .

Muchos besos,
Rafe[7]

MOVING ON

As the years passed, young Cuban refugees wherever they were located began to make a life for themselves. Many kept in touch with their foster families and also with various adults who were like substitute parents at the transit facilities. One such person was Sara Yaballi, a nurse at Matecumbe. Yaballi received hundreds of letters and cards from the young exiles, who often referred to her as "Aunt Sara." Parents of Pedro Pans still in Cuba also wrote to Yaballi, seeking her help when they were concerned about their children. One mother, for example, was waiting for a visa to come to the United States and was "very worried" that she would lose track of her teenage son before she got there. She hoped Sara could contact her son in San Francisco, where he was living with friends while applying for work with job placement agencies.[8]

While numerous Pedro Pans went into the job market after graduating from high school, many went on to

These teenage girls enjoyed their stay at a transit facility in Oregon in 1962. Their parents were still in Cuba.

college and became professionals, or they opened up small businesses and industries, or established careers in the arts or politics. Repeatedly in news articles, TV documentaries, films, and magazine stories exiled Cuban Americans are frequently cited as people who have "made it." Some representative examples include

★ Willy Chirino, the popular entertainer who created the Willy Chirino Foundation that has raised about $500,000 to help unfortunate kids

★ Gerardo Simms, assistant U.S. attorney in Miami

★ Francisco Felipe Firmat, Orange County (California) Superior Court judge

* Ileana Ros-Lehtinen, the first Hispanic woman to serve as a U.S. congresswoman
* Maria de los Angeles Torres, professor of political science at DePaul University in Chicago
* Ralph Sanchez, founder of Miami's Grand Prix
* the late Jorge Mas Canosa, a multimillionaire in the telecommunications industry and founder of the Cuban American National Foundation

Numerous Cuban Americans also succeeded as radio personalities, writers, and artists.

Whether or not they achieved fame, Cuban exiles point to their "sink-or-swim" attitude as a major factor in making the most of their talents and resources. In addition many have also benefited from a large network of Cubans in the United States willing to help each other, particularly in south Florida where 65 percent of Cuban Americans live today and in Cuban enclaves in New Jersey, New York, and California. Miguel Gonzalez-Pando, founder of the Cuban Living History Project at Florida International University in Miami explains it this way:

> The Cuban success story has too often been explained as only an economic phenomenon. Beneath the prosperous surface of their business achievements, however, lies a host of cultural, social, and political considerations that played significant roles in the early progress of the exiles. Although at first look they appeared unprepared to meet the challenge of a new life in America, Cubans had in fact brought rich traditions that had nurtured their national character for centuries. For example, their characteristic enterprising spirit, which was part of the rich

legacy they brought from their homeland, served them well in America. Unlike typical immigrants who rely mostly on the blood, sweat, and tears of their labor, Cubans tended to use their creative and entrepreneurial skills to control their own destinies.[9]

Another factor in being able to control one's own destiny was expressed by former Pedro Pan participant Jose Pimienta. During his high school years in Portland, Oregon, he was determined to fit in, to "be regular." He enrolled as a sophomore in September 1963, and "became active in high school by becoming friends with the popular kids and was voted junior class vice president." Although he experienced some prejudice when his "girlfriend's stepdad didn't want her going out with that 'Mexican' anymore," Pimienta declared that he came from "proud people. I always have thought that anyone who looks down at me because of my race or national origin has a problem themselves, not me."

In 1967, Pimienta was finally reunited with his mother and grandmother. "I never saw my father after I left Cuba," he wrote. "He was killed in a Cuban prison after being apprehended trying to escape."[10]

Executions. Escape. Exodus. Exile. All of these elements continued to be part of Cuban refugee experiences during the late 1960s and through the decades that followed.

CHAPTER 5

AIRLIFTS AND BOAT LIFTS

In spite of the missile crisis and the end of air links between Havana and Miami, an estimated 56,000 Cubans managed to emigrate to the United States between late 1962 and the end of September 1965. About four thousand, including many children, came on rafts or small boats.[1] Not everyone who tried to make the trip across the Straits of Florida arrived safely. The waters were dangerously choppy and infested with sharks; many Cubans in flimsy crafts drowned.

Castro blamed the U.S. government for these disasters, insisting that the United States had refused to allow safer travel by air between the two countries. He also declared that the U.S. government was exploiting the boat people by using them as propaganda tools—dramatizing their desperate efforts. Indeed, news stories of the time frequently referred to "Cuban refugees who risked their lives to escape the Communist government."

Whatever Castro's charges, the administration of President Lyndon Johnson, who assumed office after President Kennedy was assassinated in 1963, attempted to find a safe and orderly way to bring refugees into the

United States. Before any agreement could be reached, however, Castro apparently decided to use the refugee situation to his own advantage. Addressing a crowd gathered in the Plaza de la Revolución in Havana on September 28, 1965, he made a dramatic announcement: Cubans could leave their homeland if they had relatives in the United States asking for them.

Castro opened the port of Camarioca to any boats from the United States arriving to pick up relatives. He encouraged Cuban dissidents who wanted to leave to do so, because they were in his view "traitors" and "worms" and generally undesirable; those who remained were the patriotic ones who would "struggle for the people."

FROM CAMARIOCA TO KEY WEST

After the announcement, boats of every size and shape—including small motorboats, fishing boats, sailboats, tugboats, cabin cruisers, and luxury yachts—plowed through the rough waters to Camarioca. They were accompanied by the U.S. Coast Guard, who provided help for any craft in trouble. The boats returned to Key West, Florida, with their passengers—mothers and their young children clutching favorite toys, elderly men and women were predominant. In some cases, extended families filled an entire boat, and some trips lasted up to thirty-six hours. Most people carried only a few personal belongings. One eighty-three-year-old woman explained that she and others like her preferred to leave their "homes, clothing, and keepsakes behind in Cuba rather than continue to live with starvation, hate, and Communist propaganda."[2]

Little Moe II carried 125 refugees from Camarioca, Cuba, to Key West, Florida, as part of a boat lift that lasted only a few weeks, ending in late October 1965. During that time, several thousand Cuban refugees came to the United States.

Young men of military age—fifteen to twenty-six—were not permitted to leave Cuba. However, some escaped. Twenty-one-year-old Jesus Murgarell, for example, swam to a small boat that had left Camarioca. He reported that he risked his life rather than be forced into the Communist regime's military where he would earn $7.50 per month, be indoctrinated, and be under constant surveillance.

An estimated 200,000 refugees were expected in the United States, but the onset of the hurricane season and high seas soon forced the Camarioca boat lift to end prematurely. Yet within a few weeks several thousand (some reports say up to five thousand) Cuban refugees arrived in Key West via boats. After embarking they reported to immigration officials and were reunited with family members who were crowded along the docks waiting for them.

FREEDOM FLIGHTS

President Johnson continued his efforts to bring Cubans to the United States in a systematic manner, and on November 6, the United States and Cuba signed a Memorandum of Understanding. The agreement stipulated that the United States would provide air transportation for Cuban exiles from Varadero, east of Havana, to Miami, and that flights would begin on December 1, 1965. Persons whose immediate relatives lived in the United States received top priority.

Twice each day, these "freedom flights," as the media dubbed them, transported Cubans to Miami. Each plane carried about seventy-five to one hundred refugees accompanied by U.S. immigration and public health officials. Waiting anxiously on the observation deck of the Miami International Airport were hundreds of relatives already settled in the United States. Amid the crowd were jittery young people in the Cuban Children's Program. Social workers or administrators came with their charges and were on hand as families reunited, tearfully, joyfully, and sometimes awkwardly because parents did not always recognize their offspring who had grown up.

Roberto Halley's mother, for example, was shocked when she saw her teenage son in 1966 after four years of separation. Roberto was nine when he flew off as a Pedro Pan. He had lived at the Opa-Locka center for most of his years in south Florida and had become proficient in English; he was also a high school basketball player. A *Miami Herald* reporter described his family reunion this way:

> Tiny, attractive Mrs. Halley looked up with mock disbelief at her tall son in his Ivy League skinny tie and button-down shirt.
>
> She decided he looked like a carbon copy of his lean, good-looking father ... a scholarly man who speaks several languages and was a prominent business executive in Cuba until Castro agents arrived to shut down his bottling plant one day in 1961. [Mr. Haley] peered closely at his son. "He's a gentleman," he pronounced, beaming.
>
> "I have to keep remembering he's not my baby any more. I mustn't tell him what time to go to bed," Mrs. Halley admonished herself.[3]

Other Cuban parents expressed similar sentiments when they saw their children. Antonio Amador was seventeen years old when he was reunited with his father, and by then Amador had grown a mustache. The first words he heard from his father were: "You have to shave!"[4]

In March 1966, Mel Martinez in Orlando was also awaiting his parents. By this time, Martinez had moved to another foster home; the Youngs had taken in Eileen's mother and their home was bursting at the seams. Although the transition was heart wrenching for all, the Youngs knew that Jim and June Berkmeyer would be excellent caregivers. They had been foster parents for Mel's friend Cesar Calvet until at the age of eighteen

Calvet moved to New York City to take over the care of a thirteen-year-old sister. She had been staying with an aunt and uncle, but because Cesar was now "of age" he was expected to assume that responsibility until his parents were able to emigrate from Cuba to the United States.

Meanwhile Martinez had been carefully preparing for his parents' arrival. Like many other Pedro Pans he reversed the parent-child roles to become the "provider" of sorts. When he was reunited with his parents in Orlando, he had already arranged to get his veterinarian father a job on a large dairy farm, "a proud accomplishment," he said. He also had saved over $300 from after-school and summer jobs and gave the money to his father to buy an old car and rent a house.[5]

Omar Maden, one of the relatively small number of Afro-Cubans to fly to the United States via Operation Pedro Pan, was another refugee who planned well for his parents' exodus from Cuba. In spring 1962, Maden had been sent to a Catholic Charities program for refugees in Portland, Oregon. When the freedom flights were announced, he was a junior in high school, attending classes from 8:30 A.M. to 3 P.M. After school he went to his job as a floor cook at a local hotel, working from 5:30 to 11:00 P.M. Out of his pay that averaged about $250 per month, Maden saved the $1,200 needed to bring his parents to Portland.

Reunions took place in numerous cities across the United States, but not all were positive experiences. Some child exiles had forgotten Spanish and could not communicate with their parents without interpreters. Others had become attached to their foster parents and did not want to leave them. In some cases, children were hostile toward their mothers and fathers, believing their parents had simply abandoned them, dumped them in a foreign land. Or they resented their parents for not being able to provide the kind of home and comforts they had come to expect.

CHARGES OF FAVORITISM

In spite of some difficult family reunifications or outright rejections, Cuban communities in the United States were ecstatic that the freedom flights were underway and pitched in to help the new exiles find jobs, housing, and other necessities. The U.S. government also aided refugees by passing the Cuban Adjustment Act of 1966, which allowed special exemptions for Cubans to become American citizens; they did not have to "go through the cumbersome process required for refugees from other countries."[6]

Countless refugees expressed their gratitude to the United States for opening the door to freedom. But as the influx continued into the 1970s, non-Cubans, especially those in south Florida, increasingly complained. Some charged that the U.S. government was favoring one group of refugees over another. Others worried about overcrowded schools or about whether Communist spies were part of the Cuban influx. Older citizens, who had retired in Miami, resented the changes taking place and began to move away, farther north. They also helped pass a referendum banning the translation of various legal documents into Spanish.

African Americans in Miami were especially critical of the Cuban influx. For one thing, refugees often took many unskilled and semiskilled jobs that blacks traditionally filled, causing unemployment in the black community to rise. Blacks also "watched in anger and amazement as the 'temporary guests' became the beneficiaries of social and educational programs that the Civil Rights movement had long fought for," wrote Cuban historian María García. "For most blacks, the refugee crisis proved yet again that they were second-class citizens in their own society."7

The freedom flights brought relatively few Afro-Cubans to the United States, primarily because those given preference to emigrate were relatives of the children in exile, most of whom were white. Afro-Cubans also feared being caught in the midst of racial violence. During the 1960s, civil rights demonstrations and protests brought numerous confrontations between black citizens and police. Police harassment and attacks on blacks with clubs, fire hoses, and dogs were frequently reported in the Cuban media to illustrate that freedom was not easily achieved in the United States. Some leaders of the Black Panthers, a group espousing "power to the people," went to Cuba to speak about the black revolutionary cause, which they likened to the guerrilla war led by Castro and Che Guevera.

When Afro-Cubans emigrated to the United States, most went north to such cities as New York, Detroit, and Chicago, where they hoped to escape racist attacks. They were joined by thousands of nonblack Cuban exiles, among them members of Cuba's Chinese and Jewish populations, most of whom were merchants.

In the early 1970s, Castro began to disrupt the freedom flights, stopping them for short periods; then in the spring of 1973 he terminated the air links altogether. From the time of Castro's takeover in 1959 to the mid-1970s, more than half a million Cubans fled their homeland to the United States.

MAKING A HOME
AWAY FROM HOME

Although Cuban émigrés settled in large numbers in the Northeast, Midwest, and West, south Florida became a home away from home for the vast majority of exiles. South Florida appealed because of its climate and proximity to Cuba. In many cases, Cuban exiles who settled outside the Miami area came back. A limited survey of schoolchildren in 1965 showed that 28 percent, or more than four thousand, had lived outside Dade County for an average of fourteen months and returned.[8]

During the 1960s and 1970s, Miami became the major center of Cuban culture, particularly in an area near downtown now called Little Havana. Here newcomers could (and still can) find familiar sights—such as elderly men sitting at park tables, smoking their Cuban cigars while playing their favorite game of dominoes. Spanish-language newspapers, magazines, business and street signs, and the sounds of Cuban music are ever present.

Holidays are celebrated the Cuban way also. While Jewish Cubans and other religious groups carry on their traditions, they are in the minority. Religious celebrations reflect the Catholic majority, particularly during the Christmas season. *Nochebuena* (good night) is a Christmas Eve festivity, when relatives gather for a reunion and big dinner that usually includes roast pork, black beans and rice, and fried plantains (like bananas). Although dishes may vary, such foods are common among Puerto Ricans, Mexicans, and other Hispanic groups as well.

Perhaps the most anticipated celebration is on January 6, *Los Tres Reyes Magos* (Three Kings Day),

Costumed dancers parade during Calle Ocho, a two-week
celebration of Cuban culture in Miami's Little Havana.

the Feast of the Epiphany. This is the day children receive their Christmas gifts that traditionally come from Gaspar, Melchior, and Balthasar, the three wise men who presented gifts to the baby Jesus. A grand parade marches down Calle Ocho in Little Havana to mark the day.

Other religious celebrations include the feast day for la Virgen de la Caridad (Our Lady of Charity) on September 8. That day a flotilla of decorated boats creates a colorful display in Biscayne Bay.

Another festivity is the celebration of *quinceañersa*, the traditional birthday party for fifteen-year-old Cuban girls. This "coming-out" event has often been lavish as families compete with costume balls, limousines, and other splashy events to show off their wealth in grand style.

By the 1980s, writes historian García: "The Cuban presence permeated [Miami]. Small Cuban-owned businesses lined all the major thoroughfares." Not all the Cuban businesses remained small, however. For example, Armando Codina, a Pedro Pan who arrived in Miami in 1960 when he was thirteen, created a multi-million-dollar data processing center before he was thirty years old. He also became a major landowner and developer. He credits his success to his involuntary exile. As he explained: "I was a very spoiled kid who rode motorcycles. Everything to me was just good times and motorcycles. I had no responsibilities, no cares. I had everything I wanted. Had I not come here [to Miami], I don't know what would have happened to me. I was on the wrong track."

Codina started out his career in banking but soon went on to develop his own business, becoming a workaholic and spending seven days a week at his new company. In an interview with a *Miami Herald* reporter, he said:

> I feel so bad about what had happened to my country, but it really helped me become a better person. It taught me to appreciate more, to set my priorities for what I wanted. If I live here [in the United States] 100 years, I could not repay what this country has done.
>
> I am grateful I was given the opportunity to succeed, and I took advantage of it.[9]

That view has been repeated frequently by financially successful Pedro Pans and other Cuban Americans wherever they live. Orlando bank executive Cesar Calvet said it simply: "Hard work always pays off!"

POLITICAL ACTIVITIES

For years Cuban exiles also have worked hard to keep the cause of *Cuba Libre*, Free Cuba, an issue in American politics. Since the 1960s, many Cuban political organizations and groups have consistently argued for tough U.S. actions against Cuba, advocating everything from military invasions to strict trade sanctions. A restriction on Cuba's sugar imports by the Eisenhower administration in mid-1960 was an early embargo that has since been strengthened to ban U.S. exports to Cuba. Many Cuban Americans have long asserted that the United States should not aid the Castro regime by helping to improve its economy.

President Jimmy Carter, however, wanted to improve relations with Cuba, and after he took office in 1977 he frequently advocated peaceful negotiations between the two countries. Dozens of militant Cuban exile groups vehemently opposed Carter's policies, although a number of other exiles supported them. Among the supporters was a group of young exiles known as the Antonio Maceo Brigade who traveled to Cuba to observe the revolution in action; for three weeks in December 1977, they worked on a housing project, inspected factories and schools, and visited relatives. When they returned to the United States, the exile press denounced them as traitors in the war for Cuba's freedom and called them agents of the Castro regime.[10] The brigade was accused of filing reports with the Cuban government on Eliseo Alberto, son of a well-known Cuban poet. Even though both men supported the revolution, the government security officials coerced Alberto to spy on his own father.

In 1978, Castro issued an invitation for exiled Cubans to take part in a dialogue with his government. No U.S. officials were allowed to come. A Committee-of-75, made up of prominent exiles in the United States, Puerto Rico, Spain, and other nations, traveled to Cuba in November and December 1978 and "negotiated the lifting of travel restrictions between the United States and Cuba and the release of 3,600 political prisoners from Cuban jails."[11]

While Cuban exiles praised the release of prisoners, militant organizations stepped up their threats against anyone who would appease Castro or even travel to Cuba. Terrorist organizations bombed the businesses of those who had taken part in the negotiations, assassinated two members, and harassed supporters. Nevertheless, in spite of possible backlash, many Cuban exiles, even those who vowed never to return to Cuba while Castro was in power, took advantage of the new travel opportunities and visited their relatives in Cuba. These exiles spent millions of dollars while in their homeland, helping to boost the Cuban economy. At the same time, they also brought with them clothing, toys, books, records, and other gifts that demonstrated how well they were doing in the United States. Contact with the tourists helped spread discontent, especially among young people, and by 1980 another major exodus from Cuba had begun.

CHAPTER 6

"LOS MARIELITOS"

Although the 1960s boat lifts and airlifts were highly dramatic, heart wrenching, and often dangerous, the 1980 exodus was even more so. It began with a virtual explosion of violent actions. From May 1979 to early 1980, Cubans forced their way into Latin American embassies to gain political asylum, or refuge. A country with an embassy in a foreign land owns the territory and has jurisdiction over its compound, thus it can protect people seeking refuge from arrest and political persecution. Cubans hoped that once inside a friendly compound they could obtain visas to leave the island. To gain entry to the embassies, which were surrounded by fences or walls, they crashed vehicles through the gates. In some instances, Cuban police opened fire, wounded and killed several people, and arrested others inside the compounds.

On March 18, 1980, Hector Sanyustiz drove a bus through the gates of the Peruvian Embassy. In the bus were five other people, including a twelve-year-old boy. Guards shot at the bus, wounding Sanyustiz and one of his companions. Peruvians took them to a hospital, where a pro-Castro mob gathered outside and called for Sanyustiz to be sent to *paredón* (the wall) where Castro enemies were executed by a firing squad. "I thought for sure I was going to die, or at least go to prison for a very long time," he told a *Miami Herald* reporter in September 1998.[1] But Sanyustiz managed to escape to the United States with his wife and son, who was only five years old at the time.

When the Peruvian ambassador refused to allow Cuban soldiers to arrest his uninvited guests, Castro ordered the guards to leave the compound. This supposedly was an ultimatum to Peruvian authorities that they would not receive protection from Cuba. However, no one could predict what would happen next.

Word spread quickly throughout Havana that the Peruvian Embassy was wide open. Within a few days 10,800 people were jammed inside the protected territory, which became so crowded that there was no more room to stand or sit, except on walls or in trees. For almost a week people waited in the sun and rain, with little food and water. Finally an emigration plan was worked out between the governments of ten countries. Peru could accept only one thousand refugees, while Argentina, Canada, Costa Rica, Ecuador, France, and West Germany were able to take a total of 2,500. The United States promised to find homes for 3,500 refugees, but eventually took in thousands more from the embassy compound.[2]

A "FREEDOM FLOTILLA"

Once again Castro decided to rid Cuba of dissidents and to manipulate U.S. immigration policies. On April 20, 1980, he announced that all Cubans who wanted to emigrate to the United States, including the refugees in the Peruvian compound, were free to leave from the Port of Mariel, if friends and relatives came to pick them up. The announcement shocked Cubans and the U.S. exile community. Within hours thousands of Cuban Americans were on their way to Key West to rent or buy boats that would take them to Mariel and bring back refugees. However, when they got to the Cuban port, guards forced them to wait days for their relatives and then to take on strangers as passengers before they were allowed to leave for Key West. Some of the strangers had been released from prisons and institutions for the mentally ill.

Meanwhile, the Cuban government organized massive rallies and marches to show support for Castro. In one speech, Castro angrily declared, "He who does not have a mind to adapt to the idea of the revolution, he who does not have the heart to adapt to the effort and the heroism, we don't want them. We don't need them!"[3]

"Freedom flotillas" brought more than 6,000 refugees to south Florida during the first week, and by the first of November 1980, nearly 125,000 Marielitos, as they became known, had arrived. Among them were an estimated 13,000 to 18,000 young children and teenagers.

The trip across the Straits of Florida was the worst of nightmares for some. Boats were overcrowded, and when a storm came they were swamped with water. In one such experience a Coast Guard vessel came to the rescue of a shrimp boat crammed with thirty-seven people, but the high waves prevented the Coast Guard from getting close enough to save everyone. A survivor described the tragic scene:

Background: In April 1980, a huge crowd of Cubans took refuge in the Peruvian Embassy compound in Havana. They were seeking visas to leave Cuba.

When the shrimper began drifting away and [remaining passengers] realized they could not be picked up, the women picked up their children and threw them over the railings over to our side.

Eight or nine children were flung in the air. I caught one, a baby—about nine months old—so cold his skin was blue. And his eyes were open wide in terror.

The women on the boat looked so desperate when their ship began to drift away. They wailed in pain. I could hear their voices trail off in the darkness begging us to look after their children.[4]

CONFUSION AND CONFLICTS

The massive influx of Cuban refugees created confusion and a state of emergency in south Florida, even though federal, state, and voluntary agencies had dealt with similar waves of exiles years before. A major problem stemmed from a federal law that placed quotas on the number of refugees allowed from various countries. The quota for Cubans was 19,500, and the law stipulated that refugee status applied only to those who would suffer religious or political persecution if they returned to their homeland.

The federal government maintained that most in the Mariel boat lift were motivated by economic interests—they wanted to take advantage of job and career opportunities in the United States. Because they were not technically categorized as refugees, tens of thousands of Cubans who came on the freedom flotilla became illegal aliens, joining the ranks of thousands of Haitians in the country who did not qualify for refugee status either.

Boats that were part of the 1980 "freedom flotillas" were often overcrowded. In spite of such difficulties, by November 1, 1980, nearly 125,000 Marielitos had been transported to Key West.

To deal with the problem, the Carter administration created a new classification under the Cuban-Haitian Entrant Act of 1980, which basically meant that the Marielitos and the Haitians could remain in the United States on a temporary basis until the government determined their status. It also meant that Cuban émigrés would no longer receive special treatment from the federal government.

By mid-May 1980, President Carter called for a halt to the freedom flotillas, which were threatening to overwhelm south Florida and the nation. The boats kept coming however, and screening thousands of "entrants" was no simple matter. Four hundred U.S. Marines went to Key West to help maintain order and move Cuban refugees to various locations. A tent city of some eight hundred people went up in Miami's Orange Bowl Stadium and another near Interstate 95. Housing arrangements in Florida also were set up in three armories and at the Opa-Locka and Eglin air bases. Other centers opened on military bases in Arkansas, Pennsylvania, and Wisconsin. People were held in the centers until relatives or other sponsors could find them homes and jobs.

Photographer Jerry Sierra, who had been a refugee himself, visited Eglin in May 1980 and created a photo essay that he has since posted on the Internet. "One look at the new refugees told me their departure had not been as civil as my family's," he wrote. "I'd never seen or heard so many horror stories before. Many of them looked physically ill, and some were bleeding, or wearing dirty, improvised bandages."[5]

As the newcomers waited for weeks, many Cubans became more and more frustrated. Sierra wrote that there was an "atmosphere charged with tension and despair" in the Eglin camp, which by May 9 was filled to capacity (9,700 people). Even though there was a strong sense of community ... there was also "a level of disappointment, coupled with boredom and mixed with nervous energy." Some of the men "offered to help build the large tents, but were not allowed to handle tools. They found it difficult to stand around all day, with nothing to do but walk around the camp and watch the air force soldiers build the tents."[6]

Late in the month, hundreds of frustrated Cubans rioted at Eglin. Another riot broke out on June 1 at Fort Chaffee, Arkansas. When the public learned that criminals and the mentally ill were among the entrants, a backlash began. The media painted all the Marielitos as the "scum" of the earth, even though only a small percentage (about 5 percent) of the total were involved in violent acts. Some Cubans who had come on earlier boat lifts and airlifts were incensed and tried to distance themselves from their compatriots, fearing that their reputations as law-abiding, hardworking individuals would be tainted. However, some of these same Cuban exiles had played a major role in the Mariel boat lift, continuing to sail to the Port of Mariel to bring émigrés to the United States.

In spite of the negative publicity, some community leaders, including Monsignor Bryan Walsh who had overseen Operation Pedro Pan and Protestant Church World Service personnel who had long worked with refugees, called for more reasoned analysis of the Marielitos. Exile communities across the nation eventually began to help their fellow Cubans get settled. However, for many years the term "Marielito" was used in a derisive way to label this group of exiles, including thousands of children among them.

CHILDREN OF MARIEL

Mariel children perhaps had the most difficult time adjusting to a new life. On the boat lift they had suffered through traumatic experiences, leaving "emotional scars that set many of them apart for a long time," according to a report published by the Cuban American National Foundation.

Enrolling in school was another shock, both to students and teachers. Most Mariel children enrolled in south Florida school systems, which had to prepare for more than 13,000 children in the fall of 1980. Very few of the children knew any English, and the teachers had little or no understanding of Spanish. Classrooms were crowded, textbooks and furniture were scarce, and teachers in short supply.

American schools were drastically different from the Cuban system. In Cuba, education focused on the revolution and youngsters "learned to read with sentences about the exploits of Che Guevera."[7] Communist propaganda had convinced children that the United States was an imperialist nation bent on taking over poor nations around the world. Attitudes toward authority were different as well. Marielito children feared authority figures but did not trust them. Discipline was a major problem because children did not understand the concept of taking responsibility for their actions. They expected to be harshly reprimanded and terrorized. Another major problem was stealing, a common practice in Cuba. People frequently stole food from government storehouses just to get enough to eat.

In spite of the initial rejection of Mariel children, the schools in south Florida apparently did an excellent job of helping them to learn English and to fit into American life. Although there were school dropouts among the Marielito teenagers, most graduated from high school—some with high honors—and went on to successful adult lives. A factor in their success was not only overcoming the language barrier but also forging ahead to prove the Marielito stereotype wrong.

A CHANGING SCENE— AGAIN

Throughout the summer of 1980, President Carter with the help of Costa Rica and Great Britain tried to negotiate a more orderly transition of Cuban refugees to the United States. Carter offered to send two large ships to

Cuba to bring back refugees if the Cubans were screened before leaving. The president also hoped to find a way to return the criminals among the Mariel refugees. But Castro rejected all efforts. By the end of September 1980, Castro once more cut off the exodus and ordered all boats waiting for passengers in Mariel harbor to leave. In the meantime, the U.S. Congress passed laws to provide funds to reimburse states for the medical, social, and educational expenses incurred because of the refugee influx.

After President Ronald Reagan took office in 1981, his administration continued attempts to return "undesirables" to Cuba. No agreement was reached until mid-December 1984. The Cuban government finally agreed to take back 2,746 mental patients and criminals, and the United States promised to issue visas in 1985 to "3,000 political prisoners and their families, and to as many as 20,000 other Cubans. In the following years, visas would be issued at the rate of 20,000 annually."[8]

The United States and Cuba appeared to be on the verge of a new relationship. All that changed, however, in May 1985 when the Reagan administration started broadcasting to the Cuban people via a shortwave station known as Radio Martí. Programs were designed to spread ideas about human rights and democracy and to discuss the repressiveness of the Castro regime. Although other stations, such as Voice of America, had broadcast similar messages, Radio Martí enraged Castro. He called the station subversive and an insult to the Cuban people because it used "the glorious name of José Martí for these broadcasts."[9] To the majority of Cubans whether in exile or in their homeland, Martí is a legendary hero, a poet and journalist of the late 1800s who advocated Cuba's freedom from Spain's imperial rule.

Castro cancelled the migration agreement with the United States, banned trips by Cuban Americans to Cuba, and in short cut off all negotiations. That did not prevent private citizens from taking action. The Cuban American National Foundation and members of the U.S. Catholic Conference worked with the U.S. State Department and the Immigration Service and several other federal agencies to arrange for the release of political prisoners in Cuba. More than one hundred prisoners, some of whom had spent longer than twenty years in jail, were freed and allowed to fly to Miami on September 15, 1986. On that flight was Ramón Grau Alsina, who had played a vital role in Operation Pedro Pan and had been able to stay in touch with Monsignor Walsh through letters on tiny scraps of paper smuggled from prison. The two men met for the first time when Grau arrived at the Miami International Airport a free man.

Even as political prisoners were being released, public pressure continued for some type of migration agreement between the United States and Cuba. In November 1987 the two governments finally reinstated the 1984 accord, providing for the deportation of some "undesirable" Marielitos to Cuba and allowing a more orderly immigration of other Cubans to the United States. Nevertheless, Cuban exiles, federal and south Florida officials, and the Miami media were keeping a close watch on social and economic conditions in Cuba. They feared there would be another massive boat lift, which would bring still one more refugee crisis.

CHAPTER 7

THE
BALSEROS

It could hardly be called a massive boat lift in 1990, but early that year the number of Cubans secretly leaving their homeland began to rise. They created rafts by lashing together pieces of wood or they used rubber inner tubes, plastic bathtubs, and surfboards. Some had small homemade rowboats. Then with hardly any food or other provisions they set out, usually at night, to cross the Straits of Florida.

Cuban *balseros* (rafters) picked up by the U.S. Coast Guard increased from 467 in 1990 to more than 3,000 in 1993 to well over 21,000 by mid-1994.[1] Cuban men, women, and children risked dying in the Straits of Florida rather than continue to live under an oppressive regime. Many balseros—an estimated one out of four— never made it to the United States. As was true with such attempted crossings in the decades before, some refugees were washed into the sea by huge waves and drowned, others were attacked by sharks or died of dehydration and exposure. In some cases rafters became completely lost in the ocean, especially in the dark.

Still, thousands overcame almost impossible odds and managed to make the treacherous crossing. One ingenious man used a lightning bug—a firefly—to illuminate his compass, and the bug gave out enough light all night so that the balseros could see in what direction they were going. They landed safely in Key West where a museum that was once a refugee transit center has encased the firefly in a glass frame to mark its life-saving feat.

CHAOTIC CONDITIONS

Economic and social conditions in Cuba steadily deteriorated during the 1990s. For years Cuba's economy had been dependent on subsidies and other financial support from the Union of Soviet Socialist Republics (USSR), but with the breakup of the USSR in 1991 aid amounting to about $6 billion per year to Cuba was cut off. The U.S. Congress added to Cuba's economic woes by passing the so-called Cuban Democracy Act of 1992, which was strongly supported by Cuban exile groups working for Castro's overthrow. The new law strengthened the long-standing trade embargo against Cuba. It prohibited subsidiaries of U.S. firms based in other countries to trade with Cuba. No U.S. citizens were allowed to travel to Cuba or to send money to family members in Cuba. This law was designed, its sponsors said, as a means to bring down the Castro regime in weeks, which of course did not happen.

Throughout the 1990s Radio Martí and other stations consistently aired broadcasts urging Cubans to leave or to commit acts of sabotage against the Cuban government. Many young Cubans tuned to programs that featured exiles who had made it to the United States and were enthusiastically touting their freedom. Discontent among the young was widespread, and many secretly built their rafts hoping to escape as others had done.

Some Cubans tried to flee by way of the U.S. Naval Base at Guantanamo Bay, Cuba (established as part of the Spanish-American War agreement). Refugees hoped to find asylum there, but the Cuban government prevented access to the base from the Cuban side by erecting high barbed-wire fences, digging ditches, planting minefields, and setting up heavily manned sentry posts. Nevertheless, some desperate Cubans tried to escape by sea, boating or swimming to the naval base. In 1993 about two hundred found asylum at the base, but in the summer of that year Cuban patrol boats savagely attacked fleeing swimmers, tossing grenades and shooting at them, killing at least three, if not more. The *Miami Herald* reported:

> The attacks on swimmers in Guantanamo Bay drew especially sharp criticism because the refugees might easily have been detained without violence, U.S. officials said. "The idea of blowing up people when they are vulnerable underwater is appalling."[2]

During the summer of 1994 some Cuban groups tried to escape by hijacking boats. One group commandeered an old tugboat moored in Havana harbor. Called "13 de Marzo," the tugboat was attacked by the Cuban Coast Guard. A year later, here's how a refugee woman described the scene:

We were leaving the country on a tugboat at 3:00 A.M. when two firefighting boats approached us. They began using high-pressure hoses against us. The children were screaming. My eight-year-old daughter asked, "Why are they throwing so much water at us?" We looked behind us.

They began bumping us. That's when our boat sank. I held on to a floating body. A drowned woman. I held the body. But the waves came and then I couldn't.[3]

In its report on the tragedy, the Inter-American Commission on Human Rights (IACHR) condemned the "13 de Marzo" incident that the Cuban government did nothing to prevent. When the tugboat sank, forty-one people died, including ten minors. Noted the IACHR:

> The Cuban State not only allowed such grievous events to go unpunished, it also encourages their repetition by describing the actions taken by the crews of the boats that sunk the tug ... as "truly patriotic efforts." In fact, the Cuban Head of State said ... that "the Ministry of the Interior investigated and there was not the slightest intention to sink the [13 de Marzo].[4]

Violent incidents like the tugboat sinking became more frequent in 1994, prompting major street protests and riots in Havana in August. Once more Fidel Castro threatened to use his crafty and cynical escape strategy to get rid of malcontents, which had been so successful in previous decades. He would attempt to "demonize the exiles and the United States even as he forced them to the bargaining table in order to end the mass exodus."[5]

In several angry speeches Fidel Castro once more blamed the United States for encouraging discord and Cuban migration. He demanded that the United States stop "stimulating illegal immigration" and threatened to allow another mass exodus like the Mariel boat lift. Castro made it clear that Cubans were free to leave the island as long as they used their own craft and did not hijack or steal boats.

The U.S. government responded differently this time, declaring that the U.S. Coast Guard would stop vessels from Cuba and would not allow another mass migration to the United States. The administration of President Bill Clinton (elected in 1992) had consulted with conservative exile groups who agreed to support his actions. Clinton also hinted at a naval blockade but did not pursue such a threat since this would have been an act of war. Clinton, however, did issue a statement on August 19, 1994, denying Cubans entry to the United States. The president announced that the U.S. Navy would intercept rafters at sea and hold them indefinitely at processing centers; the first screening center was the U.S. Naval Base at Guantanamo Bay, Cuba. This was a complete reversal of a Cuban refugee policy that had been in effect since 1959.

Cuban balseros paid little attention to the rhetoric. They simply began leaving the island—by the thousands. Most were looking for a better way of life. At the same time, Haitians, too, were attempting to escape poverty and oppression and tried to get to the United States on rafts and other flimsy craft.

Although denied entry by President Clinton in August 1994, many Cubans were so desperate to leave Cuba that they tried to cross the Straits of Florida in flimsy makeshift boats.

THOUSANDS OF RAFTERS

In late August 1994 so many rafters filled the Straits of Florida that the U.S. Coast Guard and Navy had to launch a massive interception operation. Ten navy warships and more than thirty Coast Guard vessels—cutters and buoy tenders—plied the waters. They reported picking up more than eight thousand rafters in just a four-day period.

But the rafters kept coming until tens of thousands were detained at Guantanamo. Because the Guantanamo base soon overflowed, about 7,500 refugees were detained at camps in Panama for up to six months.

At first, so many refugees arrived so fast at Guantanamo that military personnel could not build shelters fast enough to house everyone. The camp had no electricity and little running water. Many refugees were forced to sleep on the ground. Food and clothing were also scarce. Tensions mounted and riots erupted.

The military was able to restore order and to eventually install electricity and sewer lines. But as the days stretched into weeks and then months of waiting, many rafters became deeply depressed, and some committed suicide or attempted to kill themselves by hanging, drinking bleach, overdosing on prescription drugs, or by cutting their wrists. Some tried desperately to go home by jumping into the sea from high cliffs or by crossing the minefields that surrounded the U.S. base—actions that brought only death.

Various groups in the United States held protests demanding an end to the concentration camps, as they became known, and filed court cases charging that refugees' human rights were being violated. Religious groups attempted to ease some of the difficulties at the camp by sending relief packages as well as by taking part in campaigns for the refugees' release.

In January 1995, Elly Chovel, who had been a 1960s Pedro Pan refugee, joined a south Florida Catholic delegation that visited Guantanamo. She and others in her group watched a nativity play performed by refugee children on Three Kings Day, "an earth-shattering experience," she said.[6] For Chovel, the play reminded her of her own childhood and being forced to leave her home and parents. But in her words, "My exodus seemed less important compared to what these people were enduring. How do we heal from this and make it better?" she wondered.[7]

To help with the healing, Chovel took two violins to Guantanamo, gifts from her father, Carlos Vilano, who has a music shop in the Miami area and is a longtime collector of violins. The gift instruments were presented to two talented child musicians at the base.

Bringing music to brighten desolate lives is just one way that volunteers helped ease what many called the nightmare of Guantanamo. The National Association of Evangelicals' World Relief program sent workers, with the consent of the U.S. government, to provide psychotherapy services, medical aid, help with English-language classes, classes in vocational training, including computer, carpentry, electronics, plumbing, and other job skills.[8] Volunteers also provided contact names in the United States for refugees who were allowed to emigrate.

In the spring of 1995 the Clinton administration announced that the United States and Cuba had signed a mutually acceptable migration policy. Under the accord, the United States agreed to accept 20,000 Cuban refugees annually, which virtually assured that refugees at Guantanamo would make up that total. Other Cuban illegal immigrants would be sent back to Cuba, but could apply for visas to the United States. Cuba agreed that returnees would not be punished and that peaceful means would be used to prevent Cubans from leaving on unsafe rafts and boats. However, Cuba frequently violated this agreement by punishing or harassing returnees.

A CONTROVERSIAL POLICY

The new U.S. policy toward Cuban refugees all but guaranteed that a controversy would result. Articles both for and against the policy appeared in numerous newspapers and magazines. Expressing strong opposition, Elliott Abrams, who was head of the State Department's Latin American Bureau in 1985, declared:

> The new policy is monstrous. This country never threw anyone back over the Berlin Wall; we never turned a Soviet Jew or Pentecostal over to the KGB; and under Presidents of both parties, we never turned a Cuban refugee over to Castro. Until Bill Clinton came along.
>
> In both moral and international legal terms, this is a departure for the United States. The Universal Declaration of Human Rights states that "everyone has the right to leave any country, including his own." This right to emigrate has been repeatedly endorsed by American Presidents and American Congresses. . . .
>
> Needless to say, we have the right and responsibility to stop Cuban government provocations like Mariel, and to use the U.S. Navy to prevent them. But to return to Cuba individuals who have risked their lives to flee its Communist system is . . . a betrayal.[9]

Members of the Cuban American National Foundation (CANF) and many older Cuban Americans living in the Cuban enclaves of Miami and in such areas as Union City, New Jersey, strongly agreed with this view. They were incensed when Attorney General Janet Reno announced that the United States would no longer automatically grant political refugee status to Cubans fleeing the island. So infuriated were some Cuban Americans that they staged protests, and CANF leader, the late Jorge Mas Canosa, called Clinton a Castro accomplice.

On the other hand, the *New Republic* editorialized that the Clinton policy was justified on both practical and moral grounds. One major consideration was the high cost of holding rafters at Guantanamo—an estimated total was at least $150 million—and the fear that another massive exodus could occur. The editorial stated that the policy was

> also justifiable in part because it does not eliminate the freedom of Cubans to migrate to the United States. It simply subjects that right to regulation, rather than to the special exemption from regulation that has existed under the 1965 Cuban Adjustment Act. Some 20,000 Cubans a year will get visas .... Considering that the entire Cuban population is 11 million, American policy will remain, as it has been, disproportionately generous.
>
> As long as the administration does not fulfill Castro's hope for a major easing of U.S. economic and political pressure, the new rules could help undermine Communist rule. Emigration to America has indirectly complemented Castro's system of political control.
>
> Comparing the prospect of a warm official reception in Miami to the risks of resistance at home, most Cubans, understandably, sought to escape—rather than to overthrow Castro. Dreams of departure absorbed the energy of the best and sharpest potential dissidents ....
>
> Clinton has clarified the options. Bluntly, the new American policy forces more Cubans to

focus their hopes and plans on bringing about democracy at home. Castro, bereft of Soviet help, cannot withstand a citizenry intent on his downfall.[10]

By the end of January 1996, the refugee camps at Guantanamo were closed and most of the Cubans held there were gradually brought to the United States. Haitians, in contrast, were sent back to their homeland, a fact that has triggered even more criticism of U.S. immigration policies and charges of favoritism for Cubans.

SETTLEMENT PROBLEMS

Once they arrived in the United States, many balseros thought their dreams of a paradise on earth would be realized. They expected to find streets paved with gold, as have many other immigrant groups before them. But most expectations of settling into a ready-made good life were dashed.

Perhaps no balseros were more disappointed than a group of 139 teenagers who crossed the Straits of Florida at various times in 1994. They came without parents or guardians, and nearly one third were high school dropouts with little respect for authority. The U.S. government handled these teenagers as a group and placed them with foster families in such states as Michigan, New Jersey, and New York, but many rebelled against structured family living and school rules. In Cuba, fourteen-year-olds were considered adults and they were not used to living by laws that control the behavior of minors, such as prohibitions against drinking and smoking. Some ran away from their new homes.

Eventually refugee workers found they had to change their settlement programs. Teenagers were placed in subsidized apartments, and some attended part-time adult education classes when not on their jobs. Those who would not get jobs or go to school received no further federal aid.[11]

Of course not all young Cuban refugees of the 1990s have had difficulties adjusting. Like earlier exiles they have learned English, found jobs, and on occasion sent messages back home about "a better life," keeping the dream alive for others who might follow them.

BROTHERS TO THE RESCUE

In spite of restrictive immigration policies, Cuban and Haitian rafters have continued to set out for Florida. According to a 1999 news report, 1,206 Haitians and 1,025 Cubans were intercepted by the U.S. Coast Guard in 1998, and in the first two months of 1999, 587 Haitians and 406 Cubans were picked up trying to reach U.S. shores.[12] By the end of 1999, more than 1,200 Cubans had been intercepted at sea. Many of the most recent refugees have been brought in by smugglers, who charge up to $8,000 per person for the trip. But some smuggling boats never arrive—they are so overloaded that they sink at sea, drowning dozens.

A group that has long assisted the Coast Guard in its efforts to prevent refugee tragedies at sea is Brothers to the Rescue. Even before the massive influx of rafters in 1994, this humanitarian group of pilots led by Jose Basulto, who had been part of a Bay of Pigs invasion

Brothers to the Rescue is a group of pilots that assist the U.S. Coast Guard by searching for refugees stranded in the Straits of Florida.

team, began search and rescue flights over the Straits of Florida. Formed in 1991, the Brothers have flown more than 1,800 aerial search missions to spot rafters in danger. Undertaking four missions each week in four to six aircraft, they have rescued more than 4,200 men, women, and children, many of them during the 1994 refugee crisis. Once the volunteer pilots spot a raft or other refugee craft in trouble, they notify Coast Guard personnel, who send a ship or helicopter to pick up the refugees. The Brothers have also dropped food and water supplies to stranded rafters and distributed leaflets in support of dissidents over Cuba.

In February 1996 several Brothers to the Rescue planes were on a search mission when they were shot down by Cuban MiG-29 planes. Four pilots were lost.

Cuba declared the Rescue planes had been in Cuban airspace, but Brothers' leader Basulto, who had flown another plane that returned safely, denied the charges. The United Nations conducted an investigation that showed the planes had been over international waters, and the UN Security Council condemned Cuba's actions.

About the time that the Brothers to the Rescue planned its ill-fated mission in 1996, a coalition of independent dissident groups in Cuba called Concilio Cubano was preparing to meet in Havana. Several months earlier the Concilio had received permission from the government for an open meeting to discuss a peaceful transition to democracy in which Cubans worldwide could participate. Its agenda also included amnesty for political prisoners and a judicial system guaranteeing human rights.

The Cuban government, however, began to harass and arrest leaders of the coalition, and officials of the Cuban Interior Ministry went to the home of the late Sebastian Arcos Bergnes, vice president of the Cuban Committee for Human Rights and a longtime activist for democracy, to inform him that the coalition would not be allowed to hold its conference. Arcos (who died in 1997) reported that the Concilio organizers agreed to postpone their meeting in order to avoid violence. On the day of the planned Concilio meeting, the Rescue planes were shot down, and many Castro critics in Cuba and in the United States are convinced that the murders of the Cuban-American airmen were one more form of retaliation against those fighting for a free Cuba.

CHAPTER 8

PROLONGED CONCERNS

The deaths of the American pilots sparked retaliation by the U.S. government. Although the Clinton administration had been trying to encourage some cooperative efforts between Cuba and the United States, the shoot down ended what had been an increasing number of cultural and academic exchanges. Direct flights between Miami and Havana were also stopped. In addition, Clinton signed the Cuban Liberty and Democratic Solidarity Act of 1996, better known as the Helms-Burton Law, which he had previously opposed. This law greatly strengthened sanctions against Cuba.

By March 1998, in the aftermath of the January visit by Pope John Paul II to Cuba, the Clinton administration announced some U.S. policy changes. Direct humanitarian charter flights to Cuba were resumed. U.S. families were allowed to increase cash payments to their relatives in Cuba. And new efforts were initiated to allow the sale of medicines, medical supplies, food, and agricultural equipment to the Cuban people. In January 1999, President Clinton broadened these policies and included a measure to expand people-to-people contacts, such as between academics and athletes. The latter measure paved the way for the Baltimore Orioles baseball team to play an exhibition game in Cuba in March 1999, and in May the Cuban national baseball team played at the Orioles park at Camden Yards.

The Cuban government has criticized the new measures, insisting that nothing has really changed in the U.S. embargo policy. That policy continues to spark debate in the United States and around the world, and a variety of humanitarian groups, some U.S. legislators, and the United Nations have spoken out against it. In his historic Cuban visit, Pope John Paul II repeated his long-held view that the U.S. embargo against Cuba should be lifted for humanitarian reasons, a belief shared by many religious leaders throughout the world.

Over the years groups have endorsed a variety of approaches for achieving democracy and human rights in Cuba. According to a March 1999 issue brief for the U.S. Congress:

> Some advocate a policy of keeping maximum pressure on the Cuban government until reforms are enacted, while continuing current U.S. efforts to support the Cuban people. Others argue for an approach, sometimes referred to as constructive engagement, that would lift some U.S. sanctions that they believe are hurting the Cuban people, and move toward engaging Cuba with dialogue. Still others call for a swift normalization of U.S.-Cuban relations by lifting the U.S. embargo.[1]

ANTI-EMBARGO ARGUMENTS

In 1996 the American Association for World Health (AAWH) sent a medical team to Cuba to investigate the effects of the trade embargo. The AAWH issued a report in 1997, declaring that "the U.S. embargo of Cuba has dramatically harmed the health and nutrition of large numbers of ordinary Cuban citizens. It is our expert medical opinion that the U.S. embargo has caused a significant rise in suffering and even deaths in Cuba."

Since passage of the Cuban Democracy Act of 1992, ships from other countries that have been to Cuba are prohibited from visiting U.S. ports for six months. "This provision has strongly discouraged shippers from delivering medical equipment to Cuba. Consequently shipping costs have risen dramatically and further constricted the flow of food, medicines, medical supplies and even fuel for ambulances," the AAWH report states, adding:

> The declining availability of foodstuffs, medicines and such basic medical supplies as replacement parts for thirty-year-old X-ray machines is taking a tragic human toll. The embargo has closed so many windows that in some instances Cuban physicians have found it impossible to obtain life-saving medicines from any source, under any circumstances.[2]

The 1999 congressional issue brief contradicts this view, however, pointing out that since 1992 the federal government has "issued 50 licenses for exports of medicines and medical equipment," and private humanitarian donations of medicines and medical equipment to Cuba have totaled $247 million. In addition, another

$2.1 billion in gift parcels of various types have been sent to the island.[3]

To learn something about the embargo and U.S. relations with Cuba, teenage reporters from Children's Express (CE) with offices in Indianapolis, Indiana, New York City, and Washington, D.C., went to Cuba in the summer of 1996. The CE team interviewed Cubans in their homes, at school, in fast-food restaurants, and at a national meeting of Pioneers, a youth organization. Boys and girls ages six to fourteen are required to join the Pioneers if they hope for a good report card grade and to be deemed ideologically correct in their views. Several of the Cuban teenagers criticized the embargo and blamed the United States for isolating Cuba from the rest of the world.

Three years later, another group of young people visited Havana and found that Cuban students still expressed concern about U.S. government attitudes toward their country. The delegation included members of the Student Exchange between Cuba and America, Inc. (SECA), founded by David Mericle and Jacob Kitzman, students at James Madison Memorial High School in Madison, Wisconsin. SECA began after Mericle and Kitzman worked together creating an extensive Internet Web site on Cuba for a national ThinkQuest contest; they won first place in the social science category. Mericle and Kitzman then went to Cuba with Global Exchange, a nonprofit group that promotes people-to-people ties around the world. They came back from their tour convinced that more North Americans should be able to travel to Cuba in order to foster an interchange of ideas and information. As a result, they incorporated SECA and set up an Internet Web site to promote their program.

In the summer of 1999 the SECA delegation of Madison students traveled to Camagüey, Cuba, where they along with Cuban student leaders and government officials laid the groundwork for a student exchange program between the two sister cities. Sister cities are created through a program established by President Eisenhower in 1956 to increase international under-standing and foster world peace by furthering global communications and exchange at the person-to-person level.

David Mericle, the president of SECA, pointed out that Cuban students have mixed attitudes about the United States:

> On the one hand, they are friendly to any U.S. visitors to Cuba and eager to talk with students from the United States. On the other hand, they are knowledgeable of how the United States has treated Cuba historically, and they realize that the United States today is carrying out a block-ade against them that deprives them of food, medicine, and much more.

Mericle noted that while "Cuban students are kind and friendly toward the United States," they also believe the U.S. government is "hateful and malicious toward them. Many Cubans, including government officials, try to rationalize this dichotomy by directing their anger and frustration exclusively toward the U.S. government and not toward the U.S. people."[4]

Tourists from the United States are, in fact, welcome in Cuba, and they are among those who call for an end to the trade embargo and U.S. restrictions on travel to Cuba. Although the U.S. government allows Americans to travel on tours to Cuba, they are prohibited from spending money there. Exceptions are made for journalists, academics, clergy, diplomats, and people with relatives in Cuba. Tourists point to the fact that Americans have spent money in other Communist nations, notably China, and argue that trade and contact with Americans might do more to change Cuba than four decades of isolation have done.

The Global Exchange Cuba Campaign has organized a number of projects with the express goal of not only lifting travel restrictions but also trade barriers, which it calls "counterproductive" and "also extremely cruel." Created in 1993, the Campaign is a network of fifty organizations that believe restrictions on travel to Cuba violate the constitutional rights of U.S. citizens.

Another part of the Campaign focuses on free trade with Cuba through an association of "progressive business and professional" people who "formed to communicate to the American public, the U.S. Congress and the Clinton Administration the desire of the U.S. business community to open up trade relations with Cuba. As other nations rush into Cuba to enjoy opportunities for investment and trade, free of U.S. competition, we remain shut out and on the sidelines. If U.S. businesses are allowed to trade with Communist countries such as Vietnam and China, why should trade with Cuba be treated any differently?" they ask.[5]

USA*ENGAGE, a coalition of approximately 700 members representing American business and agriculture, is an aggressive lobbying group working to remove trade barriers to Cuba. The coalition believes that "U.S. economic strength is integral to our nation's security and worldwide leadership. In an integrated, globalized economy, positive U.S. economic engagement—including the ability of American farmers, workers, and businesses to compete in emerging markets—is central to our own economic prosperity and to the worldwide growth of democracy, freedom, and human rights. America's values and interests are best advanced by sustained involvement in world affairs by both the public and private sectors."[6]

A long-time Illinois politician, Governor George Ryan, champions the concept that public and private sectors should work together to lift the Cuban trade embargo. He especially wants to promote the sale of Illinois agricultural products and equipment to Cuban farmers.

Illinois governor George Ryan and several business and religious leaders visited Cuba in October 1999 in an effort to open relations between the two nations. He is shown here waving good-bye to Cuban schoolchildren.

In October 1999, Governor Ryan became the first government official from the United States to visit Cuba in forty years. He led a delegation that included business people and religious leaders.

The delegation was in Cuba for five days on what was called a humanitarian mission to present more than $1 million in medical and other needed supplies. The governor also requested and gained permission from President Castro to take a seven-year-old boy with congenital liver problems to the United States for medical treatment.

By the end of his visit, however, Governor Ryan was repeatedly expressing his political views about U.S.-Cuba relations. He emphasized his antiembargo stance, saying that it had been reinforced by his talks with some Cuban dissidents as well as by his seven-hour meeting with Fidel Castro himself. Ryan told reporters that he and Castro "don't agree about philosophy on government at all, but that doesn't mean we can't talk, discuss, share ideas and thoughts about other things that might be important to his people and to ours."

The governor also made clear that he was not concerned about Cuban Americans in Miami and other cities who have condemned his visit to Cuba. "Miami is not my concern," he said. "I don't represent Miami. I represent Illinois."[7]

TRADE EMBARGO SUPPORTERS

Embargo supporters wherever they are contend that the United States should continue to try to isolate Cuba because it is one of the best means of helping to end Castro's one-party regime. "The U.S. economic embargo against Cuba may not be perfect, but neither is doing nothing," said Daniel Fisk, a former aide to Senator Jesse Helms (R-N.C.) who helped write the Helms-Burton bill, which strengthened the embargo in 1996. "U.S. policy seeks an end to the repressive state structure of Cuba," Fisk said. "Ending the embargo without significant political change remains the [Cuban] regime's No. 1 priority."[8]

Embargo supporters also believe it is immoral to deal with a government that has consistently and systematically violated human rights, a view shared by politically powerful exile leaders in the United States as well as the Coalición Cuba Nueva (New Cuba Coalition—NCC). NCC was founded in 1989 as a nonprofit organization to study how the people of Cuba can establish a political environment and make legislative reforms that will allow them to reconstruct their country after the Castro era.

Donald Trump, American multimillionaire and owner of numerous hotels and casinos, also supports the embargo and in mid-1999 wrote an article for *El Nuevo Herald* (Spanish version of the *Miami Herald*), which NCC posted on the Internet. Trump has been asked by business people in numerous countries to build casinos in Havana to cater to foreign tourists. "But to run and join those who crave doing business in Cuba would mean having to choose between substantial profits and respect for human rights," Trump wrote. He reminded readers that

> The real cause of the Cuban people's misery is Castro's economic system, not the American embargo . . . the Cuban dictator would be delighted for Donald Trump to go to Havana

and build casino hotels there . . . . Not for raising the living standards of the Cuban people. Quite the opposite. Almost all dollars would go to prop up his police state . . .

Foreign investors are not allowed to hire Cuban workers and pay them salaries. Cuban workers' wages must be paid directly to the Government. Castro then pays the workers with Cuban currency, which is worthless, and he keeps the hard currency. Under those circumstances, my investment could not benefit Cubans, and would only replace the Soviet subsidy that Castro does not receive anymore. If I opened a casino hotel in Havana, I would have to pay Castro nearly $10,000 annually for each Cuban worker that I employed . . . . Castro would pay them the equivalent of $10 a month. The rest he would use to finance the brutal system that keeps him in power and dispossesses the Cuban people of its most elementary human rights. In other words, my investment would directly subsidize the oppression of the Cuban people.[9]

Cuban Americans with avid anti-Castro convictions are keeping up the rhetoric to maintain strict U.S. policies against Cuba, and they still roundly criticize other Cuban Americans who do not share their views. They also oppose federal legislation that would allow such cooperative efforts as a news bureau exchange between the United States and Cuba. In addition, they adamantly oppose repeal of the Cuban Democracy Act of 1992 and the Cuban Liberty and Democratic Solidarity Act of 1996.

ELIAN: A PROPAGANDA "POSTER BOY"

While pro- and antiembargo forces argue, some Cubans continue to secretly leave their country and attempt to cross the Straits of Florida. In late November 1999, in what the U.S. Coast Guard said was a smuggling operation, fourteen Cubans crammed into a flimsy aluminum boat and headed toward the United States. The overcrowded boat took on water, capsized, and sank. Eleven people died.

Early on Thanksgiving Day, five days after the boat left Cardenas, Cuba, two adult survivors holding on to an inner tube floated ashore at Key Biscayne and told their story to authorities, prompting a search operation in the Atlantic Ocean. Later that day, two fishermen off Florida's coast near Fort Lauderdale found one more survivor, five-year-old Elian Gonzalez. He was the only one left, clinging to another large inner tube. His mother and stepfather had drowned when the boat keeled over.

Elian was taken to a hospital and treated for minor dehydration. Then he was released to live with relatives in Miami—a paternal great-aunt and great-uncle, Lazaro and Angela Gonzalez, and their twenty-one-year-old daughter, Marisleysis, none of whom Elian had ever seen before. The Gonzalez family in Miami declared they should retain custody of Elian because they could provide a better life for him than he would have in Cuba. But Elian's father, Juan Miguel Gonzalez, who lives in Cuba, has a job that pays a fairly good salary, and by all reports loves his son, did not agree. Juan Gonzalez insisted that his former wife did not have permission or the right to take Elian away.

Elian soon became a political pawn, "a poster boy for the anti-Castro Cuban American National

Elian Gonzalez was rescued from the ocean off the coast of Florida in late November 1999. Shown here in Miami, the young boy became a pawn in a tug-of-war between Cuba and the United States.

Foundation," which produced "4,000 blown-up pictures of Elian with the caption, 'Another Child Victim of Fidel Castro,'" as a *St. Petersburg Times* editorial explained it.[10] At the same time, the Cuban government and Elian's father and paternal and maternal grandmothers called for the boy's return to Cuba. Demonstrators in Cuba also sported Elian's picture on shirts, banners, and posters, demanding the release of the boy. Usually when a mother or father dies, U.S. law grants custody of a child to the surviving biological parent. But another federal law allows any Cuban who reaches U.S. soil the right to stay.

WHOSE CHILD IS HE?

For months, government officials, family members, church leaders, Cuban exiles in the United States, news commentators, talk show hosts, and hundreds of others across the United States expressed their views on Elian. Cartoonists pictured Elian as a political football. Candidates for political office in the United States argued over where the little boy, who turned six years old in December 1999, belonged. Elian became the subject of legal, moral, human rights, and public relations debates:

- The U.S. Immigration and Naturalization Service (INS) declared that Elian should be returned to his father in Cuba. U.S. Attorney General Janet Reno backed the INS decision.
- Gonzalez family members in Miami filed lawsuits in state and federal courts to keep Elian in the United States and let a family court determine who should have custody of the little boy.

* Members of the U.S. Congress drafted legislation that, if passed, would circumvent the INS decision by making Elian a U.S. citizen; Congress, however, did not widely support the bill.
* With the help of the National Council of Churches, Elian's Cuban grandmothers came to the United States to make their case for the boy's return to Cuba. Their emotional pleas were broadcast across the nation, arousing both intense support and angry criticism.
* Jeanne O'Laughlin, a Catholic nun and president of Barry University, offered her Florida home as a "neutral" place for the grandmothers to meet with Elian. She at first insisted that Elian's father should have custody of his son, but later declared that she had taken note of the boy's fear and anxiety in the presence of his grandmothers, and that he had bonded with his Miami family and should not be sent back to Cuba.
* Psychiatrists, psychologists, family counselors, and foster parents countered that five- or six-year-old children frequently transfer their loyalty to almost any caregiver, particularly after losing a parent and especially when they are showered (some say bribed) with gifts and much attention.
* Groups fighting for the right of Haitian and other refugees to make a home in the United States demanded to know why one Cuban child receives preferential treatment while many refugee children from other countries are not allowed to stay.
* Numerous Cuban exiles, who as children had been part of mass migrations to the United States, said they could identify with the plight of

the little boy and noted that unless a person had lived under a repressive government he or she would never understand the fight to let Elian grow up in a free society.

A RAID AND REACTIONS

While Elian Gonzalez was in the custody of his Miami relatives over a five-month period, he hardly seemed to be "free." Day after day he was shown on TV and in newspaper photos in the company of his great-uncle or other protective adults; radio and TV talk show hosts invited guests to comment on and analyze his situation; crowds gathered outside the Gonzalez home, idolizing the boy and in some cases comparing him to Jesus; Lazaro Gonzalez and his lawyers made pronouncements for the press about legal action they were taking to try to prevent the little boy's return to Cuba. In short, a circus atmosphere surrounded Elian.

Then on April 6, 2000, Elian's father, Juan Miguel Gonzalez, his wife (Elian's stepmother), and their infant child arrived in the United States from Cuba. Juan Miguel Gonzalez expected to claim his son, and six days later, Attorney General Janet Reno ordered the great-uncle to give up the temporary custody he had been granted after Elian's rescue. The Miami family defied the order and said they would not relinquish the boy; he would have to be taken by force. Crowds, they said, would form a human chain to prevent law enforcement from entering their home.

In spite of this defiance, negotiations between federal officials and the family went on for another ten days. Meanwhile tensions mounted as Gonzalez family members, neighbors, friends, politicians, including two

Cuban-American mayors, Alex Penelas of Miami-Dade County and Joseph Carollo of Miami, who took office swearing to uphold the law, declared they would not cooperate with the federal government.

In the early morning hours of April 22, Reno gave the order to take Elian. The three-minute raid, although terrifying for the boy and creating a frenzy among the relatives, resulted in Elian's apparent joyful reunion with his father, stepmother, and half-brother in Washington, D.C.

Reaction from many of Miami's Cuban Americans was fierce. Disturbances broke out, more than 350 people were arrested, Cuban flags were waved, the American flag was burned, USA posters were marked with Nazi swastikas—all in the name of American freedom and justice. Marisleysis, Lazaro, and other relatives of Elian hopped a plane for Washington and demanded to see the youngster who hours before had been in their custody. Twice they were turned away from Andrews Air Force Base where Elian and his family were housed. In two hysterical press conferences before TV cameras, Marisleysis claimed the pictures of a smiling Elian with his father and half-brother were doctored, a claim disputed by those who analyzed the photographs. She also denounced the federal government and declared that Elian needed her as a surrogate mother. She lambasted Reno, belittling the attorney general for not having children and not knowing "what being a mother is." To many observers this seemed an ironic statement for someone who, herself, has never been a birth mother.

Meanwhile, Elian and his family were moved to a more secluded place on a Maryland farm. A cousin and school classmates from Cuba, accompanied by their parents, visited with him. And as the sad soap opera

These two photographs, which were seen around the world just hours after they were taken, raised several issues beyond the images they portray. There is no doubt that the U.S. government was dismayed by the presence of a photographer in the Gonzalez house. The release of the photograph of a frightened Elian is probably what prompted the government to immediately release the second photograph showing Elian clearly delighted to be reunited with his father.

continued, so did the political fallout. Miami's mayor Carollo fired the city manager because he refused to get rid of the police chief, who was ordered by federal officials not to inform the mayor about the raid on the Gonzalez home. The police chief soon resigned, angrily accusing the mayor of being divisive. At a news conference aired on TV, the chief said: "I was bound by law, but even if there hadn't been a law, there is no way I would have let [the mayor] know about it." The chief claimed the mayor would have alerted Cuban exile leaders to the raid, which would have put many lives at risk.

Some U.S. senators and representatives held press conferences to castigate Reno and the immigration service. A congressional hearing was scheduled to question the use of force by federal agents during the Miami raid. And the "experts" from almost every segment of American life continued to present their opinions about the highly charged and complex Gonzalez case.

A minority of Cuban Americans in Miami (including another great-uncle of Elian's) supported the reunion of Elian with his father. But their voices were seldom if ever heard. Many kept quiet, fearing that at the least they would be branded as Communists and accused of being controlled by Castro and at the worst would be threatened with violent action or physically attacked.

WHAT'S AHEAD?

No one can be certain how Elian will fare in the future, wherever he lives. Nor can anyone know for sure what will happen to Cuba if Castro (now in his seventies) ever loses control. Cuban government officials and loyal supporters insist that economic reforms are under way and will be flexible enough to support their Socialist (or

Communist) ideals for a classless society that includes free education and healthcare for all. Some Cubans contend that even though people are not happy with their economic system, they are not eager to change it entirely.

Nevertheless, many Cubans in their twenties and early thirties are expressing their frustration and disenchantment with the kind of society they will inherit. "There is no future in Cuba," Betty Perez, a twenty-seven-year old law student told a Dallas, Texas, reporter. "The word 'future' has been crossed out of my dictionary."[11]

Some Cubans, however, believe they can find a future in exile, as is obvious in the case of those being smuggled out and those leaving legally. Jose Julian, for example, was in his mid-twenties when he was allowed to emigrate to the United States. According to a news report, his father, although deeply saddened by his son's decision, "sold his 1949 Plymouth for $500 to help pay for his son's visa and one-way plane ticket." At the same time Jose's father warned that the United States might not be a promised land. "Papi," the son replied, "at least there I can fight back. Here I can't even speak up."[12]

Fighting back and speaking up for basic freedoms are actions that underscore the lives of many Cuban exiles. This has certainly been shown in the Gonzalez case, even as the impassioned rhetoric of some Cuban Americans drowns out and intimidates people with opposing views, preventing them from exercising their basic freedom to speak up.

Still behind the scenes and without a public spectacle, many Cuban American exiles and dissidents within Cuba will continue to work for *Cuba Libre*. Some will continue to risk their lives for that dream.

SOURCE NOTES

INTRODUCTION

1. Juan Clark, Ph.D. "Cuba: Exodus, Living Conditions and Human Rights," on the Internet at **http://www.fiu.edu/~fcf/ juanclark.cuba/clark97.humrtscond.html** (1997).
2. Amnesty International. "Cuba: Some Releases But Repression and Imprisonment Continue" (February 15, 1999).

CHAPTER 1

1. Roger Hernandez, "Cuban Exiles Anguish Finally Makes It to PBS," on the Internet at **http://www.latinolink.com/opin-ion/opinion 98/0830orog.htm** (August 30, 1998).
2. Claude Julien, "Church and State in Cuba: Development of a Conflict," *Cross Currents* (Spring 1961), p. 186.
3. J. F. Everhart, "I Had My Property Grabbed by Castro's Men, An American Rancher Tells His Personal Story, *U.S. News & World Report* (March 7, 1960), pp. 48–49.
4. "The Case Against Castro—An Official U.S. Report," *U.S. News & World Report* (September 5, 1960), p. 65.
5. "Miami—'Refugee City'," *U.S. News & World Report* (December 5, 1960), p. 62.
6. "Tighter and Tighter Controls in Cuba," *U.S. News & World Report* (January 9, 1960), p. 16.

7. "In Cuba, Another Communistic Move," *U.S. News & World Report* (February 6, 1961), p. 8.

8. Juan Clark, Ph.D., "Cuba: Exodus, Living Conditions and Human Rights," on the Internet at **http://www.fiu.edu/ ~fcf/juanclark.cuba/clark97.humrtscond.html** (1997).

9. Alfredo Lanier, "Operation Pedro Pan's Code of Silence," *Chicago Tribune*, Commentary (January 15, 1998), p. 23.

10. Hugo Chaviano, "Cuban Parents' Fears Were Real," *Chicago Tribune*, Commentary (January 21, 1998), p. 12.

11. "The Hemisphere—Cuba," *Time* (August 22, 1960), p. 30.

CHAPTER 2

1. Monsignor Bryan O. Walsh, "Cuban Refugee Children," *Journal of Inter-American Studies and World Affairs* (July-October 1971), p. 388.

2. Cited in Monsignor Bryan O. Walsh, "Cuban Refugee Children," *Journal of Inter-American Studies and World Affairs* (July-October 1971), p. 389.

3. Walsh, p. 390.

4. Ibid., p. 391.

5. Ibid., p. 397.

6. Félix Roberto Masud-Piloto, *With Open Arms Cuban Migration to the United States* (Totowa, NJ: Rowman & Littlefield, 1988), p. 40.

7. Cesar Calvet correspondence with the author, May 1998.

8. Anne-Marie O'Connor, "Child Exiles of '60s Cuba to Reunite," *Palm Beach Post* (November 23, 1992), p. 1A.

9. Elly Vilano Chovel correspondence with the author, April 1998.

10. Jose D. Pimienta correspondence with the author, August 1998.

11. Alfredo Lanier, "Operation Pedro Pan's Code of Silence," *Chicago Tribune*, Commentary (January 15, 1998), p.23.

12. Quoted in Mike Yuen, "Children of Exile Church Program Gave Cubans Anguish, Hope," *Houston Post* (January 3, 1988), p. 1B.

13. Jose D. Pimienta correspondence with the author, August 1998.
14. Carlos Becerra interview with the author, September 1998.
15. Carlos Becerra correspondence with the author, July 1998.
16. Katherine Brownell Gettinger, "Services to Unaccompanied Cuban Refugee Children in the United States," *Social Service Review* (December 1962), p. 381.
17. Advertisement in the *Catholic Chronicle* (May 11, 1962).
18. "Refugee Cuban Children Need Homes," *Christian Century* (April 4, 1962), p. 417.
19. Walsh, p. 412.
20. Operation Pedro Pan Group, 38th Anniversary Thanksgiving Event Program (November 28, 1998).

CHAPTER 3

1. Félix Roberto Masud-Piloto, *With Open Arms Cuban Migration to the United States* (Totowa, NJ: Rowman & Littlefield, 1988), p. 2.
2. Central Intelligence Agency, *The Inspector General's Survey of the Cuban Operation*, "Conclusions and Recommendations," National Security Archive, George Washington University Web site **http://www.seas.gwu.edu/nsarchive/ latin_america /cuba/ig_report/images/co-151**
3. Ramon Grau, "Price of Freedom for Children Was High, But Worth It," *Miami Herald* (February 11, 1997), electronic version.
4. "In Cuba: Arms Pour In, Pretense Falls Away," *U.S. News & World Report* (October 8, 1962), p. 44.
5. T. T. Nhu, "Caught Between Two Worlds 'Pedro Pans,' Youngsters Airlifted From Cuba to the United States During Early 1960s, Are Trying to Piece Their Lives Back Together," *San Jose Mercury News* (April 6, 1998), p. 1A.
6. "Reglamentos," Camp Matecumbe, original in the Richter Library of the University of Miami (no date).
7. Mel Martinez interview with the author, May 1998.
8. Ibid.

9. Melita Marie Garza, "'60s Airlift Turned Kids to Victims Cuban-Americans Seek Answers" *Chicago Tribune* (January 13, 1998), p. 1.

10. Carlos Becerra telephone conversation with the author, July 1998.

11. Joe Hall, *The Cuban Refugee in the Public Schools of Dade County, Florida, Second Report January 1962–October 1962* (Miami, FL: Department of Administrative Research and Statistics, October 1962), p. 3.

12. Joe Hall, *The Cuban Refugee in the Public Schools of Dade County, Florida* (Miami, FL: Department of Administrative Research and Statistics, Supplementary Report, First Semester 1962–63), p. 2.

13. María Cristina García, *Havana USA Cuban Exiles and Cuban Americans in South Florida, 1959–1994* (Berkeley: University of California Press, 1996), p. 29.

14. Ibid., p. 30.

15. Lillian Nitcher, "They Come Alone From Cuba," *Wisconsin State Journal* (February 11, 1963), Section 1, p. 8.

16. Sara Yaballi files, Pedro Pan Collection, Otto G. Richter Library, University of Miami.

CHAPTER 4

1. Mike Yuen, "Children of Exile Church Program Gave Cubans Anguish, Hope," *Houston Post* (January 3, 1988), p. 1B.

2. Elly Vilano Chovel correspondence with the author, August 1998.

3. Carlos Becerra correspondence with the author, July 1998.

4. Carlos Becerra interview with the author, September 1998.

5. Tom Anglio telephone interview with the author, June 1998.

6. Eileen and Walter Young interview with the author, January 1999.

7. Letter to Walter and Eileen Young from "Rafe," June 19, 1995.

8. Sara Yaballi files, Pedro Pan Collection, Otto G. Richter Library, University of Miami.

9. Miguel Gonzalez-Pando, *The Cuban Americans* (Westport, CT: Greenwood Press, 1998), p. 62.

10. Jose D. Pimienta correspondence with the author, August 1998.

CHAPTER 5

1. María Cristina García, *Havana USA Cuban Exiles and Cuban Americans in South Florida, 1959–1994* (Berkeley: University of California Press, 1996), pp. 35–36.

2. Quoted in [anonymous] "'Smuggled' Exiles Resettled," *The Voice* (November 12, 1965), p. 5.

3. Quoted in Beverley Wilson, "Family Reunion," *Miami Herald* (March 6, 1966), p. G1.

4. Quoted in Karen Branch, "Pedro Pan Alumni Give $5,000 for College Scholarships," *Miami Herald* (December 13, 1991), p. 1B.

5. Mel Martinez interview with the author, May 1998.

6. Miguel Gonzalez-Pando, *The Cuban Americans* (Westport, CT: Greenwood Press, 1998), p. 45.

7. García, p. 40.

8. Joe Hall, *The Cuban Refugee in the Public Schools of Dade County, Florida, Supplementary Report February 1965–October 1965* (Miami, FL: Department of Administrative Research and Statistics), p. 3.

9. Quoted in Mary Voboril, "VOICES: How a Spoiled Kid Got on Right Track," *Miami Herald* (December 11, 1983), p. 9M.

10. Félix Roberto Masud-Piloto, *With Open Arms Cuban Migration to the United States* (Totowa, NJ: Rowman & Littlefield, 1988), p. 72.

11. Ibid., p. 76.

CHAPTER 6

1. Quoted in Fabiola Santiago, "The Cuban Who Sparked the Exodus Breaks His Silence," *Miami Herald* (September 6, 1998), electronic version.

2. María Cristina García, *Havana USA Cuban Exiles and*

Cuban Americans in South Florida, 1959–1994 (Berkeley: University of California Press, 1996), p. 57.

3. English translation in Joe Cardona and Alex Anton, ¿*Adios Patria? The Cuban Exodus*, documentary, WNET (PBS), March 11, 1999.

4. Quoted in Helga Silva, *The Children of Mariel From Shock to Integration: Cuban Refugee Children in South Florida Schools* (Washington, DC: Cuban American National Foundation, 1985), p. 8.

5. Jerry A. Sierra, "Los Marielitos: A Photo Essay," on the Internet at **http://www.grin.net/~sierra/cuba/mariel5.htm** (May 1980).

6. Jerry A. Sierra, "Los Marielitos: A Photo Essay." on the Internet at **http://www.grin.net/~sierra/cuba/mariel11.htm** (May 1980).

7. Helga Silva, *The Children of Mariel from Shock to Integration: Cuban Refugee Children in South Florida Schools* (Washington, DC: The Cuban American National Foundation, 1985), p. 16.

8. Félix Roberto Masud-Piloto, *With Open Arms Cuban Migration to the United States* (Totowa, NJ: Rowman & Littlefield, 1988), p. 102.

9. Quoted in Félix Roberto Masud-Piloto, *With Open Arms Cuban Migration to the United States,* (Totowa, NJ: Rowman & Littlefield, 1988), p. 104.

CHAPTER 7

1. Félix Roberto Masud-Piloto, *With Open Arms Cuban Migration to the United States* (Totowa, NJ: Rowman & Littlefield, 1988), p. 136.

2. Christopher Marquis and David Hancock. "U.S. Rips Cuba's 'Extreme Cruelty' Protests 3 Killings Near Base," *Miami Herald* (July 7, 1993), p. 1.

3. Mary Gray Davidson, "Cuban Exodus 1994," Common Ground radio program (March 10, 1995).

4. Inter-American Commission on Human Rights, *Victims of*

the Tugboat "13 de Marzo" v. Cuba, Case 11.436, Report No. 47/96 (October 16, 1996).

5. Holly Ackerman, "Transition in Cuba: Terms of Change," *Peace Magazine* (March-April 1997), electronic version.

6. Elly Chovel, correspondence with the author, February 1999.

7. Quoted in Liz Balmaseda, "Veterans of Pedro Pan Relive Exodus," *Miami Herald* (January 11, 1995), p. 1B.

8. Andres Tapia, "Finding Faith Behind Barbed Wire: World Relief Aids 25,000 Detainees," *Christianity Today* (April 3, 1995), electronic version.

9. Elliott Abrams, "Castro's Latest Coup, *National Review* (June 12, 1995), p. 36.

10. "Closing the Doors. (U.S. Resumes Deportation of Cuban Refugees)," Editorial, *The New Republic* (May 29, 1995), p. 7.

11. Rachel L. Swarns, *New York Times* News Service, "Hard Times, Not Paradise for Young Cubans in U.S. (September 7, 1996), on the Internet at **http://www.latinolink. com/news/0907nyou.htm**

12. "40 Haitians Missing as 2 Boats Sink," *St. Petersburg Times* (March 7, 1999), p. 1.

CHAPTER 8

1. Mark P. Sullivan, "Cuba: Issues for Congress," Congressional Research Service report (March 5, 1999), on the Internet at **http://www.fas.org/man/crs/94-005.htm**

2. American Association for World Health, *Denial of Food and Medicine: The Impact of the U.S. Embargo on Health and Nutrition in Cuba,* "Summary of Findings" (March 1997).

3. Sullivan.

4. David Mericle e-mail correspondence with the author, October 1999.

5. Global Exchange Cuba Campaign, on the Internet at **http:www.igc.org/globalex/campaigns/cuba/**

6. USA*ENGAGE, "About USA Engage," on the Internet at **http://www.usaengage.org**

7. Quoted in Rick Pearson and Laurie Goering, "Ryan Gets Cuba's OK to Bring Out Sick Child," *Chicago Tribune* electronic edition (October 27, 1999).

8. Quoted in Latinolink, "Officials: Cuba Hopes for Better Relations with U.S." (September 30, 1998), on the Internet at **http://www.latinolink.com/news/news98/0930ncub.htm**

9. Donald J. Trump, "In Support of the Embargo and the Rights of the Cuban People," *El Nueva Herald* (June 27, 1999).

10. "Politicized Custody," Editorials, *St. Petersburg Times* (December 2, 1999), p. 24A.

11. "Cuba in Evolution," special edition, *The Dallas Morning News* (September 27, 1998).

12. Quoted in Ibid.

FOR FURTHER INFORMATION

BOOKS

Bourne, Peter G. *Fidel: A Biography of Fidel Castro*. New York: Dodd, Mead, 1986.

Conde, Yvonne M. *Operation Pedro Pan: The Untold Exodus of 14,048 Cuban Children*. New York: Routledge, 1999.

Fernandez, Alina. *Castro's Daughter: An Exile's Memoir of Cuba*. New York: St. Martin's Press, 1997.

García, María Cristina. *Havana USA: Cuban Exiles and Cuban Americans in South Florida, 1959–1994*. Berkeley: University of California Press, 1996.

Gonzalez Echevarria, Roberto. *The Pride of Havana: A History of Cuban Baseball*. New York: Oxford University Press, 1999.

Gonzalez-Pando, Miguel. *The Cuban Americans*. Westport, CT: Greenwood Press, 1998.

Hoobler, Dorothy and Thomas Hoobler. *The Cuban American Family Album*. New York: Oxford University Press, 1996.

Meltzer, Milton. *The Hispanic Americans*. New York: Thomas Y. Crowell, 1982.

Triay, Victor Andres. *Fleeing Castro: Operation Pedro Pan and the Cuban Children's Program*. Gainsville, FL: University Press of Florida, 1998.

ARTICLES

Buckley, William F., Jr. "Burrowing In On the Cuban Embargo." *National Review*, August 17, 1998.

"Canada Takes in Cuban Exiles" (World Notes). *Maclean's*, March 9, 1998.

Cantor, Judy. "The Cuba Controversy." *Billboard*, August 29, 1998.

Collins, James. "Blown Out of the Sky: Cuban MiGs Down Two Civilian Planes, Further Straining Washington's Relations With Castro." *Time*, March 4, 1996.

de los Angeles Torres, Maria. "Autumn of the Cuban Patriarchs. *The Nation*, December 1, 1997.

Drummond, Tammerlin. "Turning the Beat Around: Right-Wing Cuban Exiles Suddenly Focus Their Ire On One of Their Favorites, Superstar Gloria Estefan." *Time*, October 20, 1997.

Fields-Meyer, Thomas. "To Cuba, With Love; Thirty-Five Years Later, Elly Chovel Returns To The Island She Fled As A Child." *People Weekly*, February 9, 1998.

Franklin, Jane. "Gunning for Castro." *The Nation*, December 15, 1997.

Kirk, John M. "Cuba Libre: Blending Tropical Socialism With Market Economics." *Business Quarterly*, Spring 1996.

Pemberton, Mary (Associated Press). "Cuban, American Children Play Ball in Baltimore." May 3, 1999.

Price, S. L. "What Price Freedom?" *Sports Illustrated*, March 30, 1998.

Radelat, Ana. "Aftermath of the Pope's Trip to Cuba." *Hispanic*, September 1998.

Rivers, Jordan. "A Christmas Promise." *U.S. Catholic*, December 1996.

"The Exiles' Tale." *The Economist*, April 25, 1998.

INTERNET RESOURCES

thomas.loc.gov

www.cubanet.org

www.findlaw.com

www.fiu.edu

www.latinolink.org

www.pedropan.org

wwww.seca.org

www.usaengage.org

www.usia.gov

APPENDIX

UNITED STATES– CUBAN RELATIONS 1958–2000

Adapted from *Chronology of U.S.–Cuban Relations, 1958–1999*, United States Information Agency, United States Information Service, on the Internet at **http://www.usia.gov/ regional/ar/us-cuba/cubarch.htm**

March 14, 1958—The U.S. government suspends arms shipments to the Batista government in Cuba.

January 1959—Castro's revolutionary forces seize control of Havana.

January 7, 1959—The United States recognizes the new Cuban government.

January 1959—Trials and executions of former Batista regime officials begin.

May 17, 1959—Agrarian Reform Law expropriates farmlands over one thousand acres and forbids foreign land ownership.

May 8, 1960—Diplomatic relations between Cuba and the Soviet Union resume.

June 28, 1960—Castro confiscates American-owned oil refineries without compensation.

August 6, 1960—Nationalization of U.S. and foreign-owned

property in Cuba begins following the July suspension of Cuba's sugar quota to the United States.

August 7, 1960—The Cuban Catholic Church condemns rise of Communism in Cuba. Castro bans religious TV and radio broadcasts.

October 19, 1960—United States imposes economic embargo on Cuba, with the exception of food and medicine.

October 24, 1960—Remaining American-owned property in Cuba is nationalized.

January 3, 1961—United States breaks diplomatic relations with Cuba after Cuban government demands a drastic reduction in U.S. Embassy staff.

April 17, 1961—U.S.-supported Cuban exiles invade Cuba at the Bay of Pigs.

December 2, 1961—Castro declares, "I am a Marxist-Leninist, and will be one until the last day of my life."

January 22, 1962—Cuban membership in the Organization of American States (OAS) is suspended.

February 7, 1962—The U.S. government bans all Cuban imports and reexport of U.S. products to Cuba from other countries.

October 2, 1962—U.S. ports are closed to nations allowing their ships to carry arms to Cuba. Ships that have docked in a socialist country are prohibited from docking in the United States during that voyage, and the transport of U.S. goods is banned on ships owned by companies that trade with Cuba.

October 14, 1962—The Cuban Missile Crisis begins when U.S. reconnaissance aircraft photograph Soviet construction of intermediate-range missile sites in Cuba.

October 26, 1962—In a secret communication, Soviet Premier Nikita Khrushchev agrees not to break the U.S. blockade and offers to withdraw Soviet missiles from Cuba if the United States pledges not to invade Cuba and if President Kennedy would order Jupiter missiles removed from Turkey.

October 27, 1962—Cuba downs a U-2 plane. In a letter to Khrushchev, President Kennedy proposes immediate Soviet withdrawal of the missiles in exchange for an end to the blockade. Privately, the U.S. government informs the Soviet

Union it will withdraw U.S. missiles from Turkey once the crisis ends.

October 28, 1962—Radio Moscow announces that the Soviet Union has accepted the proposed solution.

November 21, 1962—President Kennedy terminates the quarantine measures against Cuba.

February 8, 1963—The Kennedy administration prohibits travel to Cuba and makes financial and commercial transactions with Cuba illegal for U.S. citizens.

July 8, 1963—All Cuban-owned assets in the United States are frozen.

July 1964—Members of the OAS vote to enact economic sanctions and to break diplomatic links with Cuba because of its support for subversive activities in Venezuela.

October 1965—More than three thousand Cubans leave in a boat lift from Camarioca to the United States.

November 6, 1965—The Freedom Flights program begins, allowing 250,000 Cubans to come to the United States by 1971.

1966—Father Miguel Laredo is tried for allegedly assisting in the attempted escape of a Cubana Airlines engineer. In addition, priests and other clergymen are required to enter into military service.

November 2, 1966—The Cuban Adjustment Act allows 123,000 Cubans to apply for permanent residence in the United States.

March 13, 1968—The Great Revolutionary Offensive is launched, culminating in the nationalization of the remaining private sector and mobilization of manpower for agricultural production.

July 1972—Cuba joins the Council for Mutual Economic Assistance, the Communist-bloc trade association.

February 1973—United States and Cuba sign antihijacking agreement.

October 1973—Cuba sends five hundred tank drivers to aid Syria during the Yom Kippur War.

November 1974—Assistant Secretary of State William Rogers

and Assistant to the Secretary of State Lawrence Eagleburger conduct secret normalization talks with Cuban officials in Washington and New York. The talks end because of Cuban involvement in Angola.

July 29, 1975—OAS members vote to lift collective sanctions against Cuba. The U.S. government announces its intention to open serious discussions with Cuba on normalization.

August 1975—United States modifies trade embargo to allow U.S. subsidiaries in another country to trade with Cuba.

October 1975—Cuba begins deployment of 35,000 combat troops to support the Marxist regime in Angola.

December 20, 1975—President Ford ends efforts to improve U.S.-Cuban relations due to Cuban involvement in Angola and support of the Puerto Rican independence movement.

December 22, 1975—Castro declares continued support for revolutionary movements in Angola and Puerto Rico.

February 24, 1976—Under a new constitution, Castro becomes head of the government: president of the Council of Ministers, commander of the armed forces, and first secretary of the Communist party. The practice of faith or the establishment of religious organizations in opposition to revolutionary principles is prohibited.

March 18, 1977—U.S. government lifts prohibition on travel to Cuba and allows U.S. citizens to spend $100 on Cuban goods during their visits.

April 1977—Two hundred Cuban trainers arrive in Ethiopia. Cuba supports the Katangan rebellion, causing the government of Zaire to break off diplomatic relations. Cuba maintains troops in the Congo, Mozambique, Guinea, Guinea-Bissau, and Equatorial Guinea.

April 27, 1977—The United States and Cuba sign agreements on fishing rights and maritime boundaries.

September 1977—The United States and Cuba open interests sections in each other's capitals.

January 1978—Cuba begins deployment of 20,000 troops to Ethiopia.

July 31, 1978—Castro calls for the removal of U.S. bases from Guantanamo Bay.

December 1978—The U.S. government announces that the full force of the law will be used against anti-Castro exile groups who bombed the Cuban United Nations Mission, the Cuban Interests Section, and the Soviet Mission.

July 1979—Cuban-supported Sandinistas overthrow the government of Anastasio Somoza in Nicaragua.

August 30, 1979—Senator Frank Church, the chairman of the Foreign Relations Committee, announces discovery of a Soviet combat brigade of three thousand troops in Cuba.

October 1, 1979—President Carter reaffirms that troops from Cuba would not be permitted to move against neighboring countries and establishes a Caribbean Joint Task Force Headquarters in Florida.

April 1980—Ten thousand Cubans storm the Peruvian Embassy in Havana seeking political asylum. After the easing of immigration restrictions, a flotilla of refugees begins an exodus from the port of Mariel in Cuba for the United States.

May 14, 1980—President Carter demands that the Cuban government impose an orderly departure and orders a blockade to prevent private boats from traveling to Cuba to pick up refugees.

September 11, 1980—An attaché of the Cuban Mission to the United Nations is assassinated by anti-Castro terrorists. Secretary of State Muskie issues a statement terming the murder "reprehensible."

December 22, 1980—The first of several meetings between U.S. and Cuban officials to discuss the repatriation of the Marielitos occurs.

September 23, 1981—The U.S. government announces plans to establish Radio Martí to broadcast to Cuba.

April 9, 1982—Charter air links between Miami and Havana are halted by the U.S. government.

April 19, 1982—United States effectively bans travel to Cuba by prohibiting U.S. citizens from spending money in Cuba.

October 25, 1983—United States intervenes in Grenada following a leftist coup and the discovery that Cubans are being used to build an airstrip that could have been used for military aircraft.

January 11, 1984—A presidential commission on Central America reports that the Soviet and Cuban intervention in the region has created a major security problem for the United States.

July 31, 1984—U.S. and Cuban officials hold talks on migration issues.

December 14, 1984—The United States and Cuba conclude a migration pact under which Cuba agrees to accept the return of Marielitos.

January 21, 1985—U.S. bishops visit Cuba. They meet with Castro and request the release of 250 political prisoners.

May 20, 1985—Radio Martí begins broadcasts to Cuba. The Cuban government immediately jams the signal. Castro later suspends the 1984 U.S.-Cuban immigration agreement.

1986—The Cuban government begins to grant long-term visas to foreign priests and nuns.

November 19, 1987—The United States and Cuba conclude a new immigration pact that reinstates the 1984 agreement.

March 1988—The United Nations sends a team to report on the human rights situation in Cuba.

August 23, 1988—President Reagan signs a trade act that ends licensing requirements for importing recordings, printed material, and other media from Cuba.

November 1988—At the intercession of the U.S. Catholic Conference, Cuba agrees to release forty-four political prisoners.

November 20, 1989—The U.S. Treasury Department limits travel related expenses for U.S. citizens to Cuba at $100 per day.

March 23, 1990—The first test of TV Martí is launched. It is jammed by the Cuban government.

March 6, 1991—The UN Commission on Human Rights approves resolution requesting the appointment of a UN special representative to examine the human rights situation in Cuba.

May 20, 1991—In a meeting with Cuban dissidents, President Bush calls for Castro to release political prisoners and hold elections.

September 11, 1991—Soviet President Mikhail Gorbachev states that he will withdraw all Soviet troops from Cuba.

1991—The Fourth Communist Party Congress resolves to allow members of religious groups to join the party.

December 1991—Soviet economic subsidies for Cuba worth approximately $6 billion annually are terminated.

March 3, 1992—UN Commission on Human Rights approves resolution urging Cuba to cooperate with the UN special representative.

July 1992—Changes to the Cuban constitution include measures to attract foreign investment without compromising Castro's hold on power. The official designation of the Cuban government is changed from "atheist" to "secular." Religious discrimination is also forbidden.

October 15, 1992—Congress passes the Cuban Democracy Act, which prohibits foreign-based subsidiaries of U.S. companies from trading with Cuba, travel to Cuba by U.S. citizens, and family remittances to Cuba. The law allows private groups to deliver food and medicine to Cuba.

October 1, 1993—The United States and Cuba reach an agreement at the working level on the repatriation of 1,500 criminal Cuban migrants, but high-level approval is never won.

August 1994—Castro declares an open migration policy, and a new boat lift begins when 30,000 refugees set sail from Cuba.

September 1, 1994—Talks on migration open in New York City between Cuban and U.S. officials.

September 9, 1994—The United States and Cuba issue a joint communiqué agreeing to ensure that migration between the two countries is safe, legal, and orderly. The United States agrees that total legal migration to the United States will be a minimum of 20,000 per year.

May 2, 1995—The United States and Cuba issue a joint statement reaffirming their commitment to promote safe, legal, and orderly migration. Under this accord, Cubans inter-dicted at sea or who enter the Guantanamo Naval Base ille-gally are returned to Cuba provided that they do not have any protection concerns. Returned Cubans are monitored by personnel from the United States Interests Section.

October 5, 1995—President Clinton announces measures to expand people-to-people contacts between the United States and Cuba and to allow U.S. nongovernmental organizations (NGOs) to fund projects in Cuba.

November 1995—The Concilio Cubano is formed to organize the first human rights conference in which all human rights groups on the island are expected to participate.

January 1996—The Cuban government denies Concilio legal recognition. Concilio requests permission for the conference to take place February 24, 1996.

February 1996—An island-wide crackdown on Concilio Cubano begins. During the next three months more than two hundred Concilio leaders and supporters are arrested, interrogated, and harassed.

February 24, 1996—Cuban MiGs shoot down in international airspace two civilian aircraft belonging to the Miami-based group Brothers to the Rescue. Three U.S. citizens and one Cuban resident of the United States are killed.

March 12, 1996—President Clinton signs the Cuban Liberty and Democratic Solidarity (Libertad) Act, which enacts penalties on foreign companies doing business in Cuba, per-mits U.S. citizens to sue foreign investors who make use of American-owned property seized by the Cuban govern-ment, and denies entry into the United States to such for-eign investors.

July 16, 1996—President Clinton suspends enforcement of Title III provisions of the Libertad Act permitting suits to be filed in U.S. courts against foreign investors who are profiting from U.S.-claimed confiscated property. Title III itself is allowed to go into effect on August 1.

November 19, 1996—Pope John Paul II receives Castro at the Vatican. The Pope accepts an invitation to visit Cuba.

December 2, 1996—The European Union adopts the Common Position on Cuba, conditioning developmental assistance to Cuba on fundamental, democratic change.

January 28, 1997—The president releases a report on assistance the United States and rest of the international community would provide to a transition government in Cuba.

February 12, 1997—The administration approves licenses for U.S. news organizations to open bureaus in Cuba. Only CNN is allowed in by the Cuban government.

July 16, 1997—Cuban state security arrests the Dissident Working Group on charges of enemy propaganda.

January 21-25, 1998—Pope John Paul II visits Cuba.

March 20, 1998—Clinton administration announces new measures to support people of Cuba and strengthen their ties to U.S. citizens.

January 5, 1999—Clinton administration announces additional measures to support Cuban people.

March 1, 1999—Leaders of Cuba's Dissident Working Group are convicted and sentenced to prison terms nineteen months after their original arrest.

March 28, 1999—The Baltimore Orioles play an exhibition game against the Cuban all-star baseball team in Havana; the Orioles win in the eleventh inning.

May 3, 1999—The Cuban all-star team plays the Orioles in Baltimore, winning 12-6.

July 16, 1999—U.S. Secretary of State Madeleine Albright marks the second anniversary of the Cuban government's arrest of four prominent dissidents and reaffirms the U.S. commitment to a peaceful transition to democracy in Cuba.

October 23–27, 1999—Illinois Governor George Ryan and his delegation visit Cuba, and the governor meets with Cuban President Castro. Later the governor announces his strong conviction that the U.S. embargo should end. He also receives permission from Castro to bring a sick child to the United States for medical treatment.

November 25, 1999—A small boy, Elian Gonzalez, is rescued from an inner tube floating in the ocean off the Florida coast; he is a survivor of a smuggling operation to bring Cubans to the United States.

December 1999—A major international controversy develops over the custody of Elian Gonzalez.

January 24, 2000—A bill is introduced in the U.S. House of Representatives to make Elian Gonzalez a naturalized citizen of the United States.

January 26 and 27, 2000—Identical resolutions are introduced in both the U.S. Senate and the U.S. House of Representatives declaring "the sense of the Congress that: (1) Congress should not interfere with normal immigration proceedings by taking any legislative measures designed to delay the reunification of Elian and Juan Gonzalez; and (2) the Immigration and Naturalization Service should proceed with its original decision to return Elian Gonzalez to his father, Juan Gonzalez, in Cuba, and take all necessary steps to reunify Elian Gonzalez with his father as soon as possible."

April 6, 2000—Juan Miguel Gonzalez, Elian's father, arrives in the United States with his wife and Elian's half-brother.

April 12, 2000—Attorney General Janet Reno meets with Elian's Miami, Florida, relatives and orders them to surrender Elian. The relatives refuse.

April 22, 2000—Federal agents seize Elian in Miami and reunite him with his father in Washington, D.C.

INDEX

Catholic Relief Services, 31
Catholic Social Services, 52
Catholic Welfare Bureau
  (CWB), 20–25, 41, 46
Central Intelligence Agency
  (CIA), 35–36
Centro Híspano Católico, 21
Cespedes, Guillermo, 41–42
Chaviano, Hugo, 17
Chirino, Willy, 27–28, 60
Chovel, Elly Vilano, 28–29,
  51–52, 93–94
Chovel, Maria, 28–29, 51–52
Church World Service, 31
Civil Rights movement, 70
Clark, Juan, 6
Clinton, Bill, 91, 96, 101, 102
Coalicíon Cuba Nueva (New
  Cuba Coalition—NCC),
  109
Codina, Armando, 73–74
Concilio Cubano (Cuban
  Council), 8, 100
Cooper, Louise, 24
Cuba Libre (Free Cuba), 74,
  116
Cuban Adjustment Act of
  1966, 69, 96
Cuban American National
  Foundation (CANF), 83,
  86, 95, 111, 113
Cuban Children's Program,
  19, 23–25, 31, 34, 41, 66
Cuban Democracy Act of
  1992, 88, 103, 110
Cuban-Haitian Act of 1980,
  81

Cuban Liberty and
  Democratic Solidarity Act
  of 1996 (Helms-Burton
  Law), 101, 109, 110
Cuban Missile Crisis, 40–41,
  47

Eisenhower, Dwight D., 14,
  21, 35, 74, 105
Everhart, J.F., 14–15

Felipe, Francisco, 60
Fisk, Daniel, 108–109
freedom flights, 66–70
freedom flotillas, 79–81

García, María Cristina, 47,
  70, 73
Gil, Vidal, 15
Gonzalez, Elian, 111, *112*,
  113–116, *117*, 118
Gonzalez, Juan Miguel, 111,
  113,115, *117*
Gonzalez, Lazaro, 115
Gonzalez-Pando, Miguel,
  61–62
Grau Aguero, Leopoldina
  (Polita), 37, *38*
Grau Alsina, Rámon
  (Mongo), 37–39, *38*, 86
Guantanamo Bay Naval Base,
  89, 91–94, 96, 97
Guarch, George, 29
Guevara, Che, 70, 84

Haitians, 80, 81, 91, 97, 98
Hall, Joe, 46

Halley, Roberto, 66–67
Health, Education and
    Welfare (HEW),
    Department of, 31–32
Helms, Jesse, 109
Hernandez, Roger, 13
holidays, 71, 72, 73, 93

Inter-American Commission
    on Human Rights
    (IACHR), 90

Jewish Family and Children's
    Service, 31
John Paul II, Pope, 101,
    102
Johnson, Lyndon B., 63, 66
Julian, Jose, 119

Kennedy, John F., 31, 35,
    40–41, 63
Khrushchev, Nikita, 40
Kitzman, Jacob, 104

labor market, 47, 69–70
Lanier, Alfredo, 17, 29
Little Havana, 47, 71, 73
Los Tres Reyes Magos (Three
    Kings Day), 71, 73, 93

Maden, Omar, 68
Mariel boat lift, 8, 79–85, *81*
Martí, José, 85
Martinez, Melquiades "Mel,"
    43–44, 54, 56–57, 67, 68
Martinez, Rafael, 58–59
Masud, Maria, 45

Memorandum of
    Understanding, 66
Menendez, Pedro, 20–21
Mericle, David, 104, 105
Morris, Dorothy, 53
Movimiento 26 de Julio (26th
    of July Movement), 12
Murgarell, Jesus, 65

National Association of
    Evangelicals' World Relief,
    94
Nitcher, Lillian, 48–49
Nochebuena (good night), 71

Ojeda, Magda, 30
O'Laughlin, Jeanne, 114
Operation Pedro Pan, 5–8,
    19, 23–32, 34, 35, 37,
    41–45, 52, 68, 86

Park, Morton, 52
Penelas, Alex, 116
Perez, Betty, 119
Peruvian Embassy, Havana,
    77–78
Pimienta, Jose, 29, 30, 62
Platt, Orville H., 11–12
Platt Amendment, 11–12
political activities, 48, 74–76
political prisoners, 8–10, 75,
    86
Powers, Penny, 36–37

quinceañersa, 73

racism, 41, 42, 52–53

CESAR CHAVEZ HIGH SCHOOL
8501 HOWARD DRIVE
HOUSTON, TX 77017